# In Democracy's House

## Political Lessons for All Americans

Peter L. French

Orange Hat Publishing
www.orangehatpublishing.com - Waukesha, WI

For information, please contact:

Orange Hat Publishing
www.orangehatpublishing.com
603 N Grand Ave, Waukesha, WI 53186

Edited by Kristen Bratonja
Cover design by Kelly Maddern

www.orangehatpublishing.com

For Grace
and our children,
Matthew and Katherine

# *Preface*

The thoughts, images, and facts shared here were written in the years and months before the 2016 presidential election and the inauguration of America's forty-fifth president. Those more recent outcomes and the events occurring thereafter, including intense scrutiny of the efforts by a foreign power to intrude on the historic process of choosing a new chief of state, have produced drama which now tests the foundations of our democratic system. The actions by individuals charged with governing our republic have called into question the ability of those sworn to serve the people to be good stewards of the historic legacy of the United States.

A litany of documented actions of the legislative and executive branches reveals how personal and political animus and actions have become subjects of inquiry and litigation. The responses to this extraordinary behavior by a dismayed public, a cadre of dedicated public servants and a battalion of journalists have served to temper the impact of political actions that would otherwise impose greater burdens on people least able to bear the consequences of such hurtful practices and procedures.

This current reality is not chronicled here, but the political turmoil calls on all Americans to defend our democratic way of life against groups and individuals, both foreign and domestic, who would do harm to our freedom and guaranteed rights for all citizens.

The nature of current American political life is a powerful wake-up call to the reality that even a mature democracy must be constantly protected. Our democratic freedom and equality are conditions rarely provided so abundantly which may be compromised by people who fail to share such ideals. The effort to maintain our democracy against willful persons or agencies that would diminish its importance is echoed in the words attributed to Benjamin Franklin in 1787 on the last day of deliberations about the new constitution. A woman queried Franklin, "Well, Doctor, what have we got—a Republic or a Monarchy?" Franklin responded by saying, "A republic if you can keep it!" Even at the creation of our constitution there was doubt as to whether such a unique form of government could be preserved, and such nervous anxiety persists today.

To assist in clarifying the obligations of citizenship, the essays presented here offer lessons for all Americans to consider and utilize as they fulfill their responsibilities as residents in Democracy's House.

Franklin quotation from The American Historical Review, vol. 11, 1906, p 618.

iii

# *Table of Contents*

# *Introduction*

"I don't know anything about politics!" It's a useful phrase for avoiding a political discussion. You do not have to express a party preference. You can be silent about a candidate. However, it also indicates lack of awareness of the realities controlling much of your life, realities harmful to the way you want to live. Ignorance is not helpful. Knowing how politics works is important for every American in a time when issues of health, personal welfare, and community needs are important in everyday life.

Expressing an opinion is different than knowing political realities. Everyone has opinions. The mere mention of affordable health care, equal pay for equal work, and pro-choice vs. pro-life can start a discussion. The difference between having a political opinion and knowing the "nitty-gritty" of how politics actually works is important. Political knowledge requires understanding how conditions can be changed for people left out of the American dream who hope to have more satisfying lives. Politics can both reward and punish so many Americans. Ignorance is a key to being left out. Knowledge of political realities can be the crucial factor for actions to change people's lives. The challenge for most Americans is finding an orderly framework for understanding what makes political life "tick."

This book provides a framework for examining politics. It describes several dozen elements to explain many of the political realities influencing our lives. These essays are for all Americans who have little time to study politics as they work hard each day, focus on daily family needs, pay the bills, care for their children, and wonder if their lives will ever be better. It is a book for people who have not had a social studies class for a long time. Especially, it is for people who show up for their jobs, manage household budgets on limited finances, put their kids ahead of their own needs, and try to imagine a time when retirement might finally occur.

### *Living in Democracy's House*

The starting point for learning the "must know" elements of American politics is acceptance of the fact that politics is a rough business. It is often neither fair nor reasonable. It tends to favor the few at the expense of the many. It involves sharp conflicts for power and influence. Fortunately, there are provisions in our founding documents which have maintained America through foreign wars, a civil war, and decades of political strife as thirteen colonies became a nation of more than 300 million people. In all those decades, the basic conditions of political life have remained nearly unchanged despite great advances in technology and, more recently, the electronic and digital transformation in our lives.

For a complex discussion of our politics we can put aside thoughts of America's "spacious skies, amber waves of grain, and purple mountains' majesty from sea to shining sea." Instead, a more useful image is a large house, now more than two centuries old. When it was created this house had just thirteen rooms, each symbolizing one of the thirteen original colonies. During the many decades that followed, the structure expanded to fifty large rooms representing all the states. There are even extensions on the house to represent all the territories, like Puerto Rico, Guam, and the

Virgin Islands, that are also home to American citizens. Democracy's house is crowded today. We have millions of people living in this symbolic structure that has been home to generations of native Americans, settlers, slaves and immigrants. Discussion of present day politics requires knowing how the people living here are trying to get along. And most importantly, we need to understand our responsibility to keep this house in good shape so future generations of Americans can have successful lives as they are born here or arrive on the porch as newcomers and then move from room to room over the course of their days in residence.

### *Political Lessons Learned from Childhood*

The approach taken to describe aspects of political life in democracy's house is a series of short essays. These essays include ideas drawn in part from teaching generations of college students. Each essay also has a story from my own childhood of growing up in the 1940s and 1950s when America was at war in Europe and Asia and then assumed a greater role of leadership around the globe.

Those long-ago days offer an introduction to unraveling some of the mysteries of how our politics really works. The book is not a social or political history of America. It uses history for illustrations from my life to make observations about American politics. This sharing of my memories can cause all of us to recall personal images which can be knitted together to explain the larger picture of our personal political lives.

For almost forty years I began my classes by asking students to recall their earliest political memories. Generally, awareness of political life begins when we are about age nine or, in a few special cases, even a bit younger. Some of the prominent events recalled by freshmen entering college in 1965 when I began college teaching included Eisenhower's 1956 re-election that occurred when they were nine years old. For later generations of students dominant first memories included Castro's triumph in Cuba, Kennedy's election, the Berlin Wall, the Cuban Missile Crisis, the moon landing, and Carter's surprise election victory. Over all that time there were only four events between 1960 and 1990 that penetrated down into the consciousness of three and four-year old children: Kennedy's assassination, Martin Luther King's assassination, Watergate, and the attempt to assassinate Reagan.

Stop for a moment right here! Think back to your first real political memory! It should not be something your parents told you or that you read in a book. It should be an event or fact that you can recall with clarity, remembering where you were when you learned about that event. Then, try to remember how old you were when this happened. It is very likely you were between the ages of seven and eleven.

I learned my earliest political lesson a bit early, before my fifth birthday. When I was three my mom would let me play on the front porch with some strict rules. Actually, I was receiving a first lesson on the connection between freedom and responsibility, ideas absolutely vital to the way we live our lives today. That memory introduces the first essay. Other essays may encourage recall of memories that are shared by millions of people who grew up in the middle of the twentieth century. It was a time when wartime victory was achieved, soldiers and sailors came home, opportunities for education grew, and demands for equality for each American had influence on the treatment of all groups and individuals in the country. It was also a time when millions entered the middle class and, less happily, the gap between individuals of great wealth and the majority of Americans grew ever wider. The essays are presented in six sections dealing with aspects of political life that constantly occur in democracy's big, overcrowded house. The six sections are:

**Political Basics:** The first three essays teach fundamental lessons about freedom and its limits, the place of wealth in America, and the importance of being educated as a defense of the ideals of our democracy.

**Political Virtues:** Good citizenship requires knowledge of our responsibilities. Four essays focus on patriotism, equality, civic participation, and educational opportunity.

**Political People:** Moving forward from the essays about founding principles and basic virtues, four essays focus on how people's lives shape their engagement in political life. These stories include a memory of a landmark day when I was six, a childhood fascination with the old West, conversations around our family dinner table, and a big investment my parents made for my brother, my sister, and me.

**Political Practices:** As the second World War ended, my memories took on an awareness of the wider world as I read the newspapers I delivered for nearly a decade. That knowledge, combined with lessons about winning and losing in childhood games, introduced an understanding of the meaning of political power. These essays explain that how power is exercised depends on political tools, the sequences of political action, and six basic components for analyzing any complex political action.

**Political Responsibilities:** Knowing about politics reveals the imperfections in American political life. It also presents the task of proposing remedies to create "a more perfect union!" Thus, two basic themes emerge. The first defines the importance of finances for supporting the basic values of America. The second discusses how we as residents in democracy's house have the power to solve the financial shortfalls that compromise the ideals of democracy in America.

**Political Prescriptions:** The final two essays offer prescriptions for democracy's ills. The first, introduced by a classic Christmas tale, weaves simple wisdom learned in childhood into the tapestry portraying the realities of our political life. The second essay deals with two tasks vital to ensure our country will continue to flourish for generations to come.

In summation, if you can recall the lessons shared on these pages there is a likelihood a personal sense of more engaged citizenship will occur. Whether you use these lessons sparingly or extensively, America will benefit from the fact that you have a greater sense of the responsibility owed to the nation during your years of residence in democracy's house.

Part One

Political Basics

## *Don't Go Off the Porch*
### Balancing Freedom and Order

The house in North Plainfield, New Jersey, was our home for more than four decades. I was three months old when my family moved in at the end of November 1938. The dominant feature of that house was the wide porch extending across the front and halfway down one side. In the summertime the porch was screened and became an extra room where a small boy and his friends could play, especially on rainy days where it felt like being outside while protected from summer showers. On that porch, my mom taught me some basic lessons about politics.

Lesson one was the balance between how much freedom I was entitled to enjoy and how much order was needed so I would be safe. It is a condition that applies to all political life. In my childhood it was expressed in the dictum, "You can play ON the porch, but don't go OFF the porch!" There it was! I had freedom to play as I wished, but it was freedom in a defined space. It was a place with forts built out of Lincoln Logs, Lionel trains set up in figure-eight tracks, and a huge collection of well-read comic books.

Eventual remodeling caused the porch to disappear, but for more than a decade it was the first place where a grant of freedom was made and political dynamics of life revealed. If I wanted to play on the porch as a three or four-year-old I had to ask. This was different than playing in a cramped bedroom shared with my older brother or coloring at the dining room table. Going out on the porch was an act of trust offered by my mom. And in return I accepted the basic rule, "Stay on the porch!"

Mom made all the rules. As a toddler, the "porch rule" did not allow sitting on the front steps. It certainly did not allow running around on the lawn. Mom was laying down two firm political principles. First, she defined an "area of freedom," a space where it was okay to move around unsupervised as long as the rules were obeyed. Secondly, she insisted that good behavior was expected. I understood those rules. If I did as I was told there were no consequences. But going off the porch had penalties that included no porch-time for the rest of the day or even several days.

Lesson two of "porch day's politics" was learning that the "area of freedom" to be enjoyed was neither fixed nor permanent. The amount of freedom I enjoyed was flexible. It could be granted, extended, restricted, or taken away. As I grew older the "area of freedom" expanded to include our front lawn, the street where we lived, and then the surrounding neighborhood. Rules on expected behavior became more flexible. "Be home by supper time!" "Be home before dark!" "Don't go down in the woods!" "Don't play in the park alone!" All those rules were tested. Eventually, we played in the woods, had baseball games in the park, and I was constantly late for supper, but I always had a good story to explain why I was late.

I do not recall exactly when it was okay to walk the half-mile home from the West End School by myself. It must have been when I was in second grade. In kindergarten and first grade there was always my great aunt who lived with us or my brother who would walk me home. By the time I was seven, I was on my own with new rules to follow: "Come straight home!" "Change out of your school clothes!" "Play in the house!" and, eventually, "Do your homework before supper!"

What I did not fully understand was how this step-by-step introduction to expanding freedom was important in establishing order to insure my safety. That was the unspoken concern behind all of Mom's rules. Running around on the front lawn could be dangerous if a ball rolled into the street and I chased it without looking to see if a car was coming. Going alone into the woods behind the house, especially in the spring when the brook was at flood stage, had its dangers. Playing alone or with only one other friend in the park might have led to an encounter with a grown-up I did not know. Even on family outings there were safety rules: "Play where I can see you!" "Stay on the beach near our blanket!" "Only go in the water with your brother or your father!" "Don't talk to strangers walking on the beach!" Like other rules, my childhood rules restricted my freedom and made my life safer.

This balance between freedom and obeying the rules when raising children is no different than the balance existing in our communities, towns, cities, states, and country. My parents understood how rules had to be obeyed or penalties could be imposed. An early experience about obeying grown-up laws happened one evening in 1943 when there was a knock at the door. Elmer Hendel, our local air raid warden, told my dad, "Your blackout curtains are not completely closed. I can see light from the street!" Dad said he would fix them. After all, there were German submarines off the New Jersey shore, and war time fears encouraged us to do what we were told. That blackout curtain warning was as close as we got to dealing with security issues in our quiet neighborhood, but a knock on the door at night was a lesson on the bigger meaning of how following the rules and limiting freedom can keep entire countries safe.

Lesson three of "front porch politics" was learning how freedom only has value when balanced by limits. Only with limits can freedom be truly enjoyed. Mom's rules were sensible and easy to understand. I grew up safely with no limits on my creativity. I played with neighborhood kids and suffered consequences when I exceeded the limits on freedom that Mom insisted I obey. The porch on the front of the house taught me rules for a lifetime.

### *Origin of Our Ideas on Freedom and Its Limits*

The endless demand for personal freedom that bumps up against the obligation to follow the law is a conflict that shapes our history. We began as a nation by rebelling against England. We instigated a revolution to gain more personal freedoms. We were inspired by a Declaration of Independence stating each man is entitled to enjoy "life, liberty, and the pursuit of happiness." However, when freedom from Great Britain was won we faced a more difficult task. We had to figure out how a country should apply the three lessons of freedom, order, and the balance between them that I began to learn on my front porch.

The Founding Fathers attempted to place our revolutionary ideals into a formal framework guaranteeing liberties and freedom in the former thirteen colonies. The document was the Articles of Confederation, a plan that promised too much freedom. They soon realized the plan did not work. The country experienced disruptive conditions. Americans were unhappy. Businesses could not be successful when commerce crossed state lines and rules in one state contradicted rules in adjoining states.

The Articles of Confederation did not provide enough power

for the national government to guarantee stability, ensure public order, and resolve disputes between the individual states. It was somewhat like having chaos in a home where parents do not agree or have the ability to establish rules to control the kids. Families without order can fall apart. Countries that fail to establish order and respect for rules can also be in danger of turmoil. The discontent and the squabbling among the American people in those early days of our independence made it clear that new rules for maintaining order were required.

Fortunately, for our young United States and for us today a solution was found. The new nation had leaders who remedied the flaws in our national government by creating our American Constitution. It is the most exceptional statement on governing of the eighteenth century or perhaps any century, and it continues to be extraordinary today. The debt Americans owe to the creators of our Constitution is recognized in the praise of grateful generations for this model that has preserved our nation for over two centuries. The most important feature of the Constitution was its implementation of a shift from being a "radical" new independent country to a more carefully organized government while still remaining committed to extensive personal freedoms.

Our Constitution shows its authors understood that people are imperfect creatures who can selfishly pursue personal desires without thinking about the needs of others. Consequently, they created a form of government that accepts the reality of human weakness. For example, the branches of our government are balanced through a "separation of powers" between the Congress, the President, and the Judiciary. Authority and power not specifically given to the national government is reserved for the states. However, limits are placed on the power of the states as well as the national government.

When thinking about both the Declaration of Independence written in 1776 and the Constitution written a decade later, it is clear the Founding Fathers were liberal eighteenth-century thinkers. Our Declaration of Independence was a radical, liberal document when compared to the harsh rules used by monarchs and emperors in Europe. But our founding leaders were also sensible men. They appreciated the importance of order so that freedom could be preserved and the country could maintain its strength. Our government was a tool intended to be used to ensure order. This unique group of men were very matter-of-fact in their approach to defining how governing should occur. They wanted a strong national government so that business and commerce could succeed as a result of common agreement to obeying the established rule of law.

When the adoption of this Constitution was challenged because people thought it did not guarantee enough individual rights, ten amendments – the "Bill of Rights" – were added to reduce fears the new national government might unfairly limit personal liberty. Balancing the rules for defining "areas of freedom" for both individuals and states while creating a framework to support a nation where individuals could flourish is the greatest gift of the Constitution-makers.

The Constitution-makers also gave great attention to preserving maximum freedom from governmental interference. Such freedom permitted businesses to prosper without too much regulation. Agreement was provided for trade so that goods and produce could flow across state lines without difficulty. It was important to have rules that meant a product shipped from Boston to Savannah would be paid for by the customer in Georgia and the money sent back to the merchant in Massachusetts. Our Constitution was a model of "limited government" that was progressive for its time, had sound principles designed to make America run more peacefully and included principles of freedom so government did not intrude too much on people's lives.

For the Founding Fathers, this was the kind of government they wanted. It accounted for the weaknesses of human nature and had a vision that would prove helpful in changing times as the country grew and encountered new realities. However, it also contained inconsistencies that excluded many people from the blessings of freedom. Slavery was maintained. Women were excluded from the full measure of equality. It was imperfect. But, it was flexible enough so changes could be made over time.

It is unlikely those Constitution-makers could have imagined their document would one day be required to meet the needs of a country grown to more than 300 million people. The strength of the Constitution is revealed in the limited number of amendments that have been made while maintaining the principles of freedom and order for a growing population drawn from across the globe.

### Freedom and Order in Democracy's House

Americans, no matter their age, race, gender, belief, or lifestyle preference, want to live with the confidence that their freedom to work, play, gather together, speak freely, and pursue dreams will not be destroyed here in democracy's house. The house has become increasingly diverse. We must cooperate and make compromises. Living in democracy's house, we also want to feel protected by rules and regulations that will ensure our freedom is enjoyable. We can argue over the rules but still have broad agreement about what is fair in the way we are governed. We want the water clean, food healthy, travel safe, bank accounts protected, mortgages secure, and promises of support in our older years kept. These standards of freedom and governing are meant to keep us healthy and safe while leaving room to debate how best we as a country can meet the needs of all the people.

## *Thinking about Our Freedoms and Rules for Governing*

Thinking seriously about politics is hard work. Deciding how much freedom should be allowed is not easy. People have different views! One person's view of freedom may be seen by someone else as a burden. Rules are examined and re-examined. Legal cases are fought to determine just what a rule means. Judges are asked to decide the meaning of past laws and how to apply them to the twenty-first century. When decisions are made, some will be pleased and others will look for more ways to get a rule changed. This is constant. This is politics! This is what each of us must think about when deciding what we believe is the right way for America to preserve the harmony, good will, and domestic tranquility in democracy's house. As we make decisions, we ought to continually ask ourselves these questions:

**Freedom for Whom and for What?** Making political choices about an issue requires figuring out who wants what. Who wants more freedom and who wants to maintain the existing rules? And the next question to be answered is will it provide more freedom for everyone or more freedom for a just a few? And, thirdly, is it freedom to do things that would harm the well-being and health of American citizens?

**Will a Specific Action Make Me Feel Safe?** We all want to feel safe in our homes, on our streets, in our schools and businesses, and as we travel across this land. When forming an opinion about a political issue, we must ask who will be made safe. Rules that can cause harm to any group are rules to be questioned and possibly opposed.

**Will the Pursuit of Happiness Be Permanent?** Finally, in deciding what political opinions seem most reasonable, there must be judgment as to what rules will allow the most number of people to pursue their dreams of happiness – while remembering one person's idea of happiness ought not to diminish another person's happiness or freedom!

It is clear that making political choices is a tricky business! A general principle when arriving at choices is a simple one: Ask yourself if a proposed new rule to expand or reduce freedom will serve the common good while keeping us all safe. This should be the standard by which demands for expanded freedom should be measured. More specifically, new grants of freedom ought not to benefit the few, permit businesses to engage in practices that are harmful to the public, deceive individuals as to the value of products or services, or permit behavior that threatens the health and well-being of any group in the society.

This standard also applies to government when making new regulations. Regulations should serve to make the society better, assist communities to flourish, guarantee public safety, ensure products will not cause illness or injury, establish standards of performance for public agencies and institutions that serve the public.

Today, the guarantees of safety, security, and well-being for all Americans have become a more complex set of tasks than our Founding Fathers could ever have imagined. It is also clear that political choices require thought about how those choices will serve public needs. However, if each of us sets out with the intention of finding the balance between freedom and order that best serves the public interest, a good start will have been made in understanding how to make political choices in the places where we live and work.

### *Staying on the Porch*

The porch where I began to learn about freedom and order was enclosed to provide more indoor living space for a growing family. The tiny mortgage was never fully paid off until the house was sold in 1983. But, the mortgage was renegotiated a number of times to finance modern heating, new cars, and college educations. And over the years, as I learned more about politics and democracy, I realized how those precious days on the front porch made it clear that enjoying freedom depended on wisely obeying the rules that make freedom worth having.

## *Board of Freeholders*
### Why the Wealthy Win

During the summer of 1943, my mom nearly died from a wasp sting and a violent reaction to sulfa drugs. On battlefields in Europe and Asia, sulfa drugs were the miracle treatment for wounded soldiers and thousands of lives were saved because of it during horrific battles, though there was still much to learn about proper dosages. At our house on Catalpa Avenue, Mom had been wallpapering the dining room and using a trestle table on the front porch for rolling out strips of paper and applying the paste. That is where the wasp sting happened. It also marked the beginning of a summer when I began to learn more about the balance between freedom and order and who was in charge of deciding what the balance would be.

Grown-ups never tell little kids what is going on. But even a small boy who pays attention can be aware of hushed conversations and infer something serious is upsetting the adults. A lot of talk seemed to be about care for the children while Mom was in the hospital and later recovering at home. My great aunt, a trained nurse, who lived with us took care of my one-year-old sister Ellen. My brother Dave, a self-sufficient nine-year-old, had playmates in the neighborhood whose parents became babysitters during the day until Dad was home in the evenings. I was the increasingly rambunctious five-year-old who wound up going to visit Dad's four sisters, Mom's step-mother, and, lastly, to Grandma and Grandpa French's farm in Millstone, New Jersey. The stay at the farm was the longest of all these visits. It was an exciting place that offered whole new areas of freedom, even though I was still tied to strict rules about where I could and could not go. "Stay out of the hayloft in the barn! There are holes in the floor and you'll fall through!" "Play on the porch but don't go down near the road!" "Don't chase the chickens!" Grandmothers were just like mothers. But even with all of Grandma's rules, there was still so much space to explore around the farm.

The Amwell Road farm was different from the "old farm" at Blackwell's Mill where my dad grew up. It was a small farm providing needed additional income. Grandpa's real job was painting houses. The farm was the last one in Somerset County where the French family had farmed since before the American Revolution. And the day was not far off when even that farm would be sold as my grandparents moved closer to one of Dad's sisters. But in that hot wartime summer of 1943, it was a special place for me. There was no one to supervise me closely during the day as Grandpa was away working and Grandma was in the house, mostly in the kitchen. I could wander through rooms upstairs and down, out to the barns, the garages, and the equipment shed. I could be on my own.

There was one place I was not allowed to go. Grandpa's office! It was a small room just off the kitchen with a huge roll-top desk and lots of books and papers. Grandpa would sit there in the evenings after supper to read and write. It was more office space than a small farmer and house painter really needed, and I eventually learned it was more than a personal office.

One afternoon, Grandpa came home early for supper because

it was the night of his "big meeting." That was all I was told. Actually, I was more excited by Grandpa's promise to wake me up before dawn the next morning so I could help with the "morning work," which meant feeding the pigs, chickens, and cows, and watching Grandpa do the milking.

The purpose of those monthly "big meetings" was explained to me during the next three years of summer visits to the farm. Each summer was different, as Grandma gave me chores to do that included collecting eggs from the hen house, weeding the vegetable garden, and picking blackberries that grew on the lane that ran down to the meadow. The conversation also changed as I had lots of questions, but my grandparents were patient with their answers. I learned Grandpa's monthly "big meeting" was the gathering of the Somerset County Board of Freeholders. Walter W. French, my Grandpa, was secretary to the Board. He kept the minutes of the meetings and recorded the decisions on how the county was governed.

The term freeholder is "old-timey" sounding and a reminder of the way things have worked in New Jersey since colonial times. Today, New Jersey is the only state that still uses this term to describe the way counties are governed. Other states have Boards of "Commissioners" or "Supervisors" to govern their counties.

### *Where Our Ideas About "Rule by the Rich" Come From*

As set down in the New Jersey Constitution of 1776, men who "freely held property or wealth" valued at fifty pounds were "freeholders" and entitled to vote. To be elected to a Board of Freeholders, a candidate was required to have property or wealth valued at one thousand pounds and thereafter at least five hundred pounds to stand for re-election. That may not seem like a lot of money, but in colonial times it was a small fortune just to have enough money to be a voter and a big fortune to be able to be a candidate. When the American Revolution commenced, the "freeholder" class in the colonies had flourished and produced men of substantial wealth as well as thousands of small farmers and businessmen. More importantly for the study of politics, the voting requirements based on wealth established the principle that voting and office-holding was based on economics.

To support the idea of wealth as a standard for elected office, there was a prevailing philosophical belief in England and in all the colonies that because these freeholders had a bigger stake in the orderly running of communities, freeholders ought to be in charge. Unlike a landless, poor, or itinerant person, these freeholders were considered entitled to a significant role in political life as voters or, if wealthy, as political leaders who could decide how counties were organized and governed.

The concept of tying political influence to wealth was based on the philosophic idea that the "wisest and best" ought to govern. It created a combination of wealth, wisdom, and suitability to govern as a foundation for rule. Men who were financially successful logically became the freeholders. For Somerset County in central New Jersey, the historic term is preserved today and reminds us that since our country's earliest days wealth conferred a special privilege in the process of governing.

Placing responsibility in the hands of men who valued political and social calm as the sensible way to achieve a stable environment in which business could flourish and economic enterprises grow was considered ideal by the ruling freeholders. The adoption of the American Constitution established a national foundation for providing order while reserving certain powers for the individual states. The freeholders in the states made this approach to governing work at all levels of government.

What the Constitution did not resolve was the conflict between the founding ideals in which *all* men were to be considered equal and the establishment of second-class citizenship for those who did not have the fifty pounds needed to vote or the hundreds of pounds needed to be a candidate for elected office.

With rare exceptions, the wealthy have always had a dominant role in how governing is done. The people in power have preferred a government providing maximum freedom to make money and sufficient order so that society is not disrupted. It was the foundation of a sense of privilege that still prevails and has now grown more pronounced in the twenty-first century as the gap in wealth between the middle class and the rich grows ever wider.

### *Wealth and Equality in Democracy's House*

Many of the struggles in our history are the continuing efforts to provide maximum freedom to all citizens. Those struggles include ending slavery, extending voting rights to women and African Americans, and providing access to the ballot box for all eligible citizens. The continuing conflict between the privileged wealthy minority and the majority of the population explains the persisting tension between those with financial interests who demand fewer limits on economic action and those who demand more government regulation to protect the well-being of each and every citizen.

Thoughtfully considered, most of today's Americans are less interested in more freedom then they are in a dependable structure so there are things that can be counted on each day. The majority of Americans may not know the details of politics, but they know when something does not seem right. And it is their limited understanding of the intricacies of politics that has offered an opportunity for people of influence, especially the wealthy, who prefer fewer government regulations. The rich and powerful seek to persuade Americans that too much government is the cause of the public's collective worry. These powerbrokers argue that less government regulation would be better. It is an argument that reveals how too many Americans have forgotten what the Founding Fathers quickly learned in the first years of independence: Freedom is only truly free when we live in a society where there is dependable order. The wealthy argue having less government would reduce taxes and mean everyone could keep more of what they earn. It is an idea that directly links to the businessmen and farmers who once served as the freeholders of Somerset County when our republic was founded.

### *Thinking about Wealth and Equality in America*

My brother, my sister, and I grew up as members of "the missing generation." We were not compared to the "greatest generation" or the post-war "baby boomers." We were depression-era babies where from infancy, we were more cautious because our parents were fearful of risk when all around them was the evidence of what a true depression economy looked like. We were taught to obey rules, work hard, and be cautious about the future.

My dad began a tradition of writing birthday letters to his sons when David was born, letters that shared both worry and doubt about the future. He was less diligent about writing letters to me, and there are only four letters preserved from the years when I lived at home. Excerpts from those messages to a small child show the emphasis placed on acting responsibly, taking school seriously, and being apprehensive about the world I inhabited and would inherit. The fears, anxieties, and obligations threaded throughout those birthday messages were beyond my understanding at the time, but they describe the atmosphere of our family life.

August 6, 1942:

*"Dearest Peterkins,*

*...tomorrow you will be four years old. And in only one more year you will be able to follow David off to school when the bells call all the little boys and girls away from their play in September. Before that happens you have a whole year before you begin to 'put on the harness' of going to school."*

August 6, 1943:

*"My dear little 5 year old-*

*In just a few hours now you will be celebrating your 5th birthday. Sometimes as I look at you and David when you are at play and envy you all the time and the years and the opportunities that lie ahead of you... (Y)our whole life has been colored by events you couldn't possibly understand or be held accountable for. Yet you and David and Ellen, all your little cousins and millions of other little boys and girls will be forced in later years to take up the heavy load this war is placing on your little shoulders even as you continue your boyhood school days."*

August 6, 1946:

*"My dear Son-*

*Just a short letter to let you know that mommy and I haven't forgotten the day you came to us... Only eight short years ago and yet many people have lived a whole lifetime in those few years... Yes, Pee-Bee you have lived through eight very exciting, dangerous and stimulating years, but looking back I would wish for years which held less promise of things, very dangerous and heartbreaking things, to come."*

August 6, 1953:

*Dear Son-*

*It just doesn't seem possible that 15 years have slipped away so fast... looking back time seems to have telescoped into a few terribly short years. However, such a great deal has been crowded into those years and we have lived at such a terrific pace this old world seems to resemble a bloke that has just gotten over a weekend binge."*

This caution made us more orderly in school and obedient at home. It made us less likely to challenge authority and to do our homework every night. We approached our future with a special awareness of what life was like when resources were short and things were rationed. We knew the country had lived through a terrible economic time and was still fearful of such conditions coming again. Our goal was to work hard and, hopefully, prosper just a bit. As children we had little idea how wealth was distributed.

Today, in our later years, it is people of my generation who are stunned as we look at a country that has endured such financial disarray and watched carefully assembled bank accounts and investments built over a lifetime be washed away in an electronic instant. Those losses are the result of unwise judgments by people who never experienced a real depression. We worry about our grandchildren and the longer-term future of the country. We know there is a continuing conflict between freedom and order. But we do not necessarily want less order. What we want is order that works. We still want clean water, safe food, safe air travel, good education for our children, and safe healthcare. If we were to list all the things that government does that we would willingly give up, we would be hard pressed to say what government services ought to end.

Today, what is less routinely accepted by the majority of Americans is that the old freeholder mentality may not serve the majority of Americans in a positive way. Too many actions have been taken over the past three decades to deregulate how banks, insurance companies, land developers, mining companies and chemical industries are permitted to conduct their activities. Just the examples of financial loss occurring in the first years of the twenty-first century by banking practices in the mortgage industry have provided a sense of how important the constraints imposed on businesses during the Depression in the 30's helped keep the whole country safe. Most importantly, those restrictions on businesses practices in the 1930's helped protect a growing middle class as it cautiously built resources for millions of households while their children played and learned in democracy's house.

We now realize that the wealthy in America may not have knee-breaches or powdered wigs, but they have the same motivation as their forefathers. They want just enough government so business is uninterrupted, but not so much government as to restrict engaging in risky schemes even experts do not fully understand. This results in threats to the carefully assembled assets of the "greatest generation," the "missing generation" and the now retiring "baby boomer generation." Even the much younger millennials are discovering the realities of a government less able to protect its interests.

The rise of modern recklessness by the wealthy has widened the gap between the very rich and the majority of the American people. The historic notion that wealth is a sound basis for determining who are the best qualified to govern still influences American lives. Wealthy people exercise enormous influence and control over politics. Knowledge of how our politics works must accept that basic fact. It is the determining condition that compromises the ideal of equality for the vast majority of citizens who hope productive lives will provide a place in a vibrant middle class.

Years would pass before I fully understood how politics from the earliest days of our nation still preserves the philosophic, historical, and operational reality of a system in which wealth has a disproportionate influence on how the country is governed. When that realization arrived, the Amwell Road farm had long been sold and the roll-top desk auctioned off. But the discovery of Grandpa's position as secretary to the Somerset County Board of Freeholders was the beginning of the lessons about the controlling position of wealth in America. In those long-ago days the papers in Grandpa's office recorded how freeholders controlled the wealth of Somerset County.

## *Logansville*
### Education for Equality

My mom graduated from high school in 1921. She needed
a job. Her dad was not in good health. Money was tight. Mom
knew what she wanted to be. She wanted to be a teacher. When
the story was told and re-told in our home, usually around the
dinner table, the way in which a teaching job was arranged was
not made entirely clear, but Mom got a job as an untrained teacher.
She did not become just *a* teacher. She was hired as *the* teacher in
a one-room schoolhouse in Logansville, a village tucked away in a
rural corner of Hunterdon County, New Jersey. For a small salary
plus room and board provided by a local family, Mom became the
teacher of the eighteen children spread over twelve grades at the
Logansville School.

In all the re-tellings of Mom's "Logansville Year," there were
few details of how the teaching was done, but Mom admitted she
cried herself to sleep almost every night until Christmas, nearly
overwhelmed by the challenges of trying to teach all twelve
grades. Two of the students, both girls, were nearly as old as Mom
and constantly wanted to know how old she was and if she had
a beau. It was a year that demanded guts and determination, but
Mom saw it through until June.

After Mom's Logansville adventure, she enrolled in a teacher
training program at Montclair Normal School with the confidence

that she was a teacher who could face anything a classroom might present. The Permanent Normal School Certificate issued on June 20, 1924 certified Constance Isabel Hadden, granting her "a permanent license to teach and to supervise teaching in the Kindergarten and any branch or department of the first four years of work exclusive of Kindergarten," and signed by the State Commissioner of Education. She retired in 1968, a much beloved primary school teacher for generations of young children. Her mantra was always "You have to get them started right!"

A puzzling question I have about Mom's year in Logansville is what did those kids learn during the long months from September until June? The little ones surely acquired reading skills for the first time, helped by the older children. And the older students probably got better at reading. Basic math skills also likely improved, although math was not one of Mom's strengths. Handwriting surely became more legible with lots of penmanship exercises. There might have been a bit of science, although science was not Mom's strength either.

It is likely that considerable time was devoted to American history and social studies, with a focus on public events and holidays. There might have been a pause for Columbus Day, and a lot of attention given to ceremonies on November 11, Armistice Day, which was the third anniversary of the end of the Great War in Europe. Perhaps at least one person in the village of Logansville had served in France. The tradition of wearing little poppies on Armistice Day was just beginning, and the class may have learned to recite the poem "In Flanders Fields." In February, there could have been a time set aside for Washington's birthday, and with so many thousands of Civil War veterans still alive, Lincoln – the Great Emancipator – probably had a birthday celebration too, as he was popular in northern states. At the end of May there was Memorial Day to honor the fallen of the Civil War as weather turned warm and students looked forward to summer vacation. What surely happened at the Logansville School included the opening exercises at the start of each school day when the students recited the pledge of allegiance to the flag, remained standing for a reading from the bible and, perhaps, bowed their heads for a short prayer. No day passed without remembering we were, "one nation, indivisible, with liberty and justice for all."

It was a tribute to the citizens of Logansville that learning was so important that they were willing to trust a very young, untrained teacher with the responsibility of educating their children. Their action was a tiny example of the national commitment to the teaching of young people across the country in thousands of one-room schools. Done well or poorly, those schools were the places where millions of children were introduced to ideas about how their country was organized. As generations of youngsters learned to read, write, and "cipher," they acquired abilities so they could one day make their lives like those of past generations of people seeking to rise to the level once enjoyed only by the freeholders. In those little school houses like the one in Logansville children could begin to dream of success that would turn them into farmers and businessmen who would be respected throughout their communities and beyond.

Along with those dreams of future achievement, they also absorbed the basic skills of citizenship, learning a bit about the importance of voting, the right to participate in community life, and the right to have a say in the way Logansville made choices about people's lives. Perhaps there was time spent on the passage of the Nineteenth Amendment to the Constitution in August 1920, which gave women the right to vote just a year before Mom showed up in

Logansville as the new teacher. This was a big change in American politics. It was a "teaching moment" for emphasizing the importance of education in preparing young people to be active citizens, a condition that is a fundamental requirement of democracy.

My dad was educated in the one-room school in Millstone, New Jersey, a basic building with an outhouse and lots of wood stacked up for the winter months. It was a long walk from the farm to school, but he would start early so he could check his trap line both coming and going. The muskrats he caught were for his spending money. One morning he found a skunk in one of his traps and mistakenly believed he could get that skunk out of the trap without getting sprayed. He was wrong! The teacher sent him home. That same teacher was remembered as a formidable disciplinarian who, according to Dad, once threw a student out an open window. No one talked back, but they did learn. And it was there in his one-room school that his lifelong interest in history, especially in the Civil War, was developed.

Today, the one-room schools of Mom and Dad's youth are decaying monuments to the way America once taught its children. Occasionally they can still be found in small towns where some have been made into private homes or small businesses. The rest fall quietly to ruin. Their purpose has been fulfilled as one-room schools fade from the national consciousness. America fails to recall the importance of those humble efforts in public education where citizenship was learned and the great documents of our history read. They performed the task of teaching about the enduring broad commitments to individual freedoms that slowly expanded the degree of equality for all citizens, as the passage of the Nineteenth Amendment affirmed.

Public education was and is the means for overcoming

the notion that only the wisest and best as measured by wealth should be governors. Public education created the possibility that ordinary citizens could have the skills, the wisdom, and prudence of good judgment to participate in governing. Education was the key to accepting the idea that all citizens had vested rights in how they were governed and a personal responsibility for participating in governing. The lesson was clear; the right to participate in governing should not be measured or restricted by wealth. Building school houses across America offered the means to redeem the promise that all are equal and none should be more privileged than others before the law.

How did such a change in our ideas about wealth and governing come about? In the early 1800s on both sides of the Atlantic, the debate about who ought to be educated generated the belief that government had a responsibility to provide for public education. Slowly, government-funded public education emerged as a solution for correcting the illogical thinking of the freeholder mentality, which preferred government managed by the privileged few. Public education created opportunities for everyone to gain knowledge and acquire perspective about how to make sound decisions as to how their communities ought to be governed. It was a short and reasonable step to translate that theory into the practical action of creating public schools in every community to provide education for all.

For America, the idea of making education widely available can be seen in the Northwest Ordinance, rules for settlement of the lands in the upper Midwest that would become the states of Ohio, Indiana, Illinois, Michigan, Wisconsin, and Minnesota. Those rules required each section of land to reserve space for construction of a school with an adjoining wood lot so the school could be heated during the winter months. Education in America was to be within walking distance as it was in Logansville and Millstone.

And, as public education became essential for training Americans in the responsibilities of citizenship, it also served to shift thinking about the broader responsibilities of government for the people. After all, the model of government provided by our Founding Fathers was for small or limited government. They firmly believed that "the government that governs best, governs least!" In many ways, government was considered a necessary evil to maintain order, collect revenue to finance governmental operations, and ensure tranquility for the smooth operation of business. The demand for public education, however, changed all that.

By building schools, government was given something innately positive to do. It was tasked with improving people's lives through education. Having taken up the productive action of providing public education, a logical basis was established for government to do other constructive activities. This dramatic shift was part of the beginning of modern "progressive liberalism," a liberalism that sees government as having obligations beyond just ensuring order and maximizing individual opportunities.

Eventually this revised progressive thinking came to dominate political action in the latter half of the nineteenth century, as millions acquired the knowledge, skills, and confidence to write and speak out about the broad interests of the majority of Americans. As the number of eligible voters grew, political leaders had to listen to what the people were demanding. Competing issues arose with regards to how the nation should accommodate a growing population. People wanted better working conditions, shorter work weeks, protection for children from harmful labor conditions, improved healthcare, and eventually, care for the elderly and infirm. With progressivism as a guiding philosophy, political leaders had lots of topics to consider in making new rules and regulations. It was the basis of the enlarged government we know today.

This shift in political thinking was also the basis of conflicts in governing America in the twenty-first century. There are political interests, particularly economic and business interests, which, like their forbearers, are essentially small-government people who want less government regulation. They prefer a government with minimal infringement on economic activity and limited government spending on areas like healthcare, education, safety, and a whole range of services that protect the lives of individual Americans. These small-government people wish to pay as little revenue as possible to support government social programs.

In the fall of 1921, during the first year of President Harding's administration, the eighteen students in the Logansville school were taught by an incredibly young and uncertain Miss Hadden. They had no understanding that their attendance in that tiny school in Hunterdon County made them part of the tradition that created an educated citizenry. They were part of a liberal tradition that within two decades would produce the Social Security system to assist the impoverished and elderly in the depths of the Great Depression, an innovation that benefited those students in their old age and inspired Medicare and Medicaid to ensure the healthcare of the "Greatest Generation," the "Silent Generation" and the "Baby Boomers."

### *Education for Citizenship in Democracy's House*

We must all realize that public education teaches the fundamentals of citizenship, which are basic to our democratic way of life. That learning is a bulwark against economic forces which seek to impose rules that would deprive Americans of enjoying healthy lives, full measures of personal liberty, and opportunity for diverse pursuits of happiness.

Today, however, in democracy's house, the teaching of civics or social studies has diminished importance in school curricula. Too many schools spend less money on training in citizenship. If a school budget fails to pass and produces threats that sports programs might be eliminated, a new vote is taken and sports and other extra-curricular activities are retained. But if elimination of courses on civics or social studies is proposed, cuts in these programs are too often made with hardly a murmur of protest.

Too many young people and their parents have minimal knowledge of how government works, how laws are passed, and how elections are conducted. The public is not attentive to how political leaders perform or take note as those leaders pursue their various interests. Making everyone able to serve with "the wisest and best" judgment to contribute to our democracy should be the standard for all school boards and school administrators. Without this belief and its realization in practice, a key condition of our democracy is weak and can be damaged if stronger forces make changes in rules that are not in the interest of the common good.

Whether schooling takes place in tiny rural communities, elegant suburban schools, or in crowded urban places, Mom's mantra first laid down in Logansville nearly a century ago is true today. If we are going to have a sure defense against threats to our democracy, public education must be ever attentive to the adage, "You have to get them started right!"

Part Two:

Political Virtues

# The MacArthur Medals
## Patriotic Obligations

When school opened in 1943, my brother announced he was going to win a prize for collecting newspapers to support the war effort. His goal was a ton of newspapers. I was the "helper" as we pulled a wagon through the neighborhood, knocked on doors, hauled the paper home and dumped it in the shed attached to the back of the house. I got to put my thumb on the string as knots were tied for each bundle of paper. The shed was soon full, and more bundles were stacked against the back of the house. One Saturday morning, a big truck rolled into the driveway and pulled onto the back lawn. Some big men loaded all the collected paper. We soon learned the goal had been reached. My brother had collected nearly two tons of newspaper. I had helped.

Months later, on a warm spring morning at the West End School, the weekly assembly was held on the playground. My brother and some of the other kids in the 4th, 5th, and 6th grades were lined up along the first base line of the ball field. All the other grades were spread around to watch the ceremonies. There was a Bible reading followed by the pledge of allegiance. The Principal, Mr. Harris, made a short speech and introduced a man in uniform who had lots of medals on his shirt. He told everyone what a great thing had been done in collecting all the newspapers to help fight the war. The highlight of the day was when the soldier walked down the line of the kids on the first base line, shaking their hands and placing a small medal dangling from a red, white, and blue ribbon around each boy's neck. My brother and the other boys had received the MacArthur medal for contributing to the war effort. They were young heroes in service to America.

In those days, every kid at the West End School was able to contribute to the war effort by buying war bonds. We brought in dimes and nickels each week that were placed in a wallet-sized cardboard folder. My classmates and I watched as our collection of coins built up to five dollars. Then Ms. Whitehall, my kindergarten teacher, or Ms. Scholnick, my first grade teacher, did the paperwork so each kid in the class got a war bond.

We talked about the war frequently as we drew pictures of planes with stars on the wings shooting down planes with zeroes on the wings. We all knew a tune from the 1939 Snow White movie, to which we sang our revised refrain: "Whistle while you work, Hitler is a jerk, Mussolini is a weenie and the Japs are worse!" On the way to and from school, we would carefully step on the cracks in the sidewalk and say, "Step on the crack, break Hitler's back!" Even kindergartners could be patriots.

Learning the responsibilities of being patriotic were part of the routine in every classroom. The daily exercises each morning included the Pledge of Allegiance, with only one change in the 1950's when the words "under God" were added. We also had the Bible reading, which I recall being heavily devoted to the Book of Psalms. Our teachers performed the readings until we got to the third and fourth grades, when members of the class were picked to do the Bible readings. While the war raged in Europe and the Pacific, those daily school activities taught us how to be good citizens. We did not know there was a whole curriculum for social studies in grades one through twelve. Each year students were supposed to absorb the values of respect for authority, how laws were made, how the government worked, and appreciation for how special America is.

At home, those lessons in citizenship were reinforced by Mom and Dad. In my birthday letter from 1943 Dad wrote:

*Now, this seems like so much preaching to you right now I know, but let's look at it from another angle. Your war savings, stamps and your war bonds and all the scrap metal you help collect is helping some soldier – who only a few short years ago was celebrating his 5th birthday – do a great big job on the other side of the ocean. Either in Europe or in the South Pacific where we are fighting the Japanese some soldier boy is making it possible for you to keep on enjoying a life your daddy and mommy had the good fortune to enjoy when they were 5 years old.*

*The soldiers, our fliers, our paratroopers, our marines and our sailors are saying – some with their lives – that this land of ours is just right for little boys and we don't want any 'bullies' coming over here to change it. They are fighting for your right to have a nice peaceful home, a nice school to go to where you can be taught everything without fear of stepping on someone's toes, a church where you can go to sing songs and worship God as you please. They want you to be able to work without having someone tell you what to do and how long you must work. They are even fighting for your right to play, to get dirty, to go fishing, to climb trees, to jump in heaps of leaves in the fall and roll snowballs in winter.*

Growing up in New Jersey made it easy to study the beginnings of our country because big chunks of the American Revolution were fought where we lived. From the front steps of the West End School, I could see "Washington Rock" in the Watchung Mountains, a lookout from which Washington kept track of the British as the American army moved south from New York to a more secure position across the Delaware River at Valley Forge. School trips were arranged to Morristown to see the historic encampment at Jockey Hollow State Park. We knew the story of Molly Pitcher, the heroine of the Battle of Princeton. And less than a mile from my house, on Front Street across from the A&P where we shopped, was Washington's Headquarters, which served briefly for an army on the move. The Revolution was all around us. It helped us understand that winning independence from England had been hard work.

### Patriotism in Our Time

Today, patriotic activities by little kids are not as evident. The government has not mounted a drive to buy war bonds to support our troops on far-off battlefields or the needs of veterans who have returned from war with challenging disabilities. Kids have not been asked to collect paper or scrap metal to contribute to the war effort. There is no draft of young men and women into the armed forces. We have an all-volunteer military. Thousands of Americans have died in more than a decade of foreign wars, but only occasionally

42

do we see a soldier or marine in dress uniform passing through an airport carrying a precious symbol of sacrifice, a flag folded in a triangle revealing just the stars. That warrior in dress uniform is engaged in a solemn duty called the "Patriot Detail." He or she is bringing the profound thanks of a grateful nation to grieving loved ones of a man or woman who has fallen overseas.

It is also rare to see the little banners with a simple silver star hanging in the windows of homes to tell us someone in that home is proudly serving the military. And having grown so used to what seems like permanent war, we do not see the banners with a gold star that in the war of my childhood signified a soldier, a sailor, or a marine had perished in combat and the family was in grief.

When I was a toddler, the country was slowly recovering from the worst effects of a national depression, and the call to arms defined our patriotic duty. There were shortages and rationing we accepted as necessary to support the war effort. Lawns were plowed to create "Victory Gardens!" Our victory garden alongside the house provided corn, peas, green beans, lima beans, onions, tomatoes, lettuce, strawberries, and the dreaded asparagus. If you did not eat your asparagus, you did not get strawberries for dessert. To provide food for fall and winter, vegetables were canned, grapes became grape jelly, and bundles of onions were hung in the cellar above baskets of potatoes. On our kitchen table, everyone had an individual jar of sugar to use on each morning's bowl of oatmeal because sugar was rationed. Our family's war effort was made up of doing small things in a big cause!

Today, we see little evidence of Americans being called upon to support overseas war efforts. Here at home our military is centered on bases where all-volunteer forces and their families carry the burden of endless deployments, each warrior dedicated to protecting comrades while often uncertain about the larger purpose of their courageous efforts. The financial costs of war are born by borrowing from abroad so no one, not even small children in primary school, can learn basic obligations of service in the cause of patriotic duty.

World War II was fought by those we call the "greatest generation." Now those warriors from battles in Asia and Europe pass away by the hundreds each day. Their surviving children, grandchildren, and great grandchildren can only be puzzled by a nation where the patriotism once expected of all of us seems diminished. There are no twenty-first century versions of the MacArthur Medals being presented on playgrounds across America.

It is easy to imagine that if a call had been issued on September 12, 2001 asking Americans to invest in their country by buying a new version of "Victory Bonds" to finance the "War on Terror," the government might have raised billions of dollars in weeks. America was not asked, as our leaders clung to a bi-partisan notion that war could be fought on the cheap. It apparently did not occur to them that if we really want to prevail as a country, we need the equivalent of stubby-legged kindergartners doing their part collecting materials to support the nation's needs and giving their nickels and dimes for war bonds, so their future will not be a debt owed to other countries.

### *Citizenship and Patriotism in America's Democracy*

A personal sense of citizenship is important. It can be taught in school. It can be learned through volunteering in causes greater than our own personal needs. It can be affirmed by celebrating heroism that is found even in the small places in American life. Each of us must remember what it has inspired in the past! Think about what you can do that is similar to hauling a wagon through a neighborhood asking strangers for old newspapers that were shredded for use as insulation in the flight jackets worn by airmen piloting planes over Europe.

Patriotic obligation and service can be done quietly by practicing the basic skills of citizenship: reading newspapers, attending meetings, displaying the flag on national holidays, registering to vote, and actually voting! It can also be practiced when singing the "Star Spangled Banner" as it ought to be sung with the reverence of a hymn, loudly and clearly with no hint of embarrassed mumbling. It is not a rock tune!

If citizenship and patriotism are practiced each day, we become more conscious of the vital balance between freedom and order in our daily lives. Our patriotic acts make us mindful of the responsibility to preserve equality for all Americans. Democracy's greatest threat occurs when too much power is placed in too few hands. It is our challenge to emulate past generations in defense of guarantees of equality to all Americans. We must accept that knowing about politics is a patriotic responsibility in defense of our nation's values.

# *Sunday School*
## Discovering Democracy's Needle

In our house, Sunday school was required. No excuses accepted. Saturday night was bath night so you would be ready on Sunday morning to put on your "church clothes" and your best pair of shoes. During the war years, I had three pairs of shoes. Sunday shoes, school shoes, and play shoes. Each time a new pair of shoes was bought they became the new Sunday shoes. The old Sunday shoes became school shoes, and school shoes became play shoes. Putting on our best clothes meant church was important. Being dressed and ready on time was also important or Dad would get upset.

From the time I was very small, there was always a place for me in Sunday school, beginning with the nursery class. By the time I was seven, I was accumulating those little awards for perfect attendance. They were given out on Children's Sunday in June. It began with a first-year pin, followed with a second-year wreath to go around the pin. After that, there was a little bar attached below the wreath. The last bar I received was for "ten years" of perfect attendance. My senior year in high school I had a girl friend who was a Methodist, so I missed some Sundays at the Grant Avenue Presbyterian Church. No eleventh medal! This record of perfect Sunday school attendance was accumulated at a Presbyterian church, which we began attending during the war to save on gasoline; it was closer than the Dutch Reform church.

For all those years, Roland Bahnsen was the minister, and my Sunday school teachers were Mrs. Bahnsen, Miss Gray, Mrs. Ogren, and my dad. Dad taught the high school classes. That was not easy for me. He expected the homework readings to be done and he expected me to be prepared to answer questions. He liked things orderly, gave carefully prepared lessons, and did not like interruptions. Inevitably, there came a day when he threw Charley Busnack and me out of the class for talking, not paying attention, and being unprepared. He wasn't wrong.

Thinking back, it is hard to remember the specific lessons learned in all those years of church beyond the importance of being a decent person, having expectations for living a Christian life, and feeling a sense of renewal at Christmas and Easter time. I never formally joined the Church as a youngster but was confirmed in the Presbyterian Church in my first year of college because of an extraordinary preacher, Liam Davies, whose sermons were inspirational for a college freshman away from home.

My attachment to church life, while showing up every week, singing in the choir, and doing the required activities, was not unpleasant. What I did not realize was that the Bible was my first book about politics. Reading the Bible and listening to Sunday school stories teaches a lot of basic truths about political life, even if Sunday school is focused on religious values. Awareness of the political content comes as we grow and gain understanding of how people really behave.

The way Sunday school hides or does not often focus on the political realities of the Bible is not necessarily intentional, but the following Sunday school story translates easily from religious roots to a lesson for understanding the challenges of fulfilling national ideals in a land where inequality is so pervasive.

## Democracy's Needle

The tale of a rich man having as little a chance of gaining the Kingdom of Heaven as a camel passing through the "eye of a needle" was silly to me when I was small. Even if I thought of mom's big darning needle with its large "eye," I could not make sense of the story because no one explained what "the eye of the needle" actually meant. It would have been better if just a few details had been provided.

Even as small children, we could have understood that at the entrance to ancient cities, which were protected by high walls, there were massive gates that swung open in the day time and closed at night to protect all the people in the city. We could also have understood how those ancient people realized that a good citizen could be caught on the road as night fell, and would be unable to reach a city or town before the gates swung shut. To offer protection to the latecomer, a number of those huge gates had a smaller door built into them, an opening that the late traveler could squeeze through. But if the traveler arrived on a camel, no exceptions were made for the animals. The camel could not squeeze through the small gate. That gate was called "the eye of the needle." The camel had to remain outside for the night. Having such an explanation for the "needle's eye" would have helped the Bible lesson make more sense.

Applying this Sunday school lesson to American politics, many of us accept the words of the Pledge of Allegiance that we are "one nation under God!" We say this in our blessings that precede eating, and in daily prayers at home and in our churches, synagogues, and mosques. Yet we hardly pause to consider the biblical injunction of denied salvation if an individual fails to share his or her wealth. Our historic ideal of equality is routinely compromised as the wealth of individuals expands its reach and creates ever greater divides between the extraordinarily rich and the majority of our society.

This contradiction between our democratic faith, with its promise of equal treatment for all, and the continued controlling influence of the freeholder legacy, with its emphasis on wealth, is well understood. We Americans are a people who give generously to our churches, colleges, and universities; medical research; the arts; land preservation; and in times of great need, to those who have been disadvantaged by disaster or natural calamities. Often, it is our various religious faiths that inspire our acts of stewardship. To the extent that the wealthy give to the needs and interests of our society, there is well-deserved recognition of such generosity. But one great difference remains. Gifts by the wealthy do not impoverish them as they choose who or what shall be the recipients of their gifts. Those voluntary gifts are of the donor's choice. They may not touch the more profound needs of those in our society who would benefit greatly from such gifts.

In a nation "under God," this Sunday school parable of camels and needles needs to be learned again, with private yachts substituted for camels. For the small number of people who control so much of the wealth, there needs to be acceptance of a revised parable to realize the ideals of our democracy. That modified parable can be:

> *It is easier for a yacht to pass through the "eye of equality in democracy's needle" than for a wealthy man to be a good steward of America's democratic ideals.*

Our public religion of democratic equality obliges us to create conditions within our land whereby all citizens can envision the opportunity to realize their individual talents and abilities. Many steps have been taken to realize that obligation, from the end of slavery to the extension of the right to vote. Many of those steps have been shaped by a commitment to economic equality, such as fair employment practices, employer-based medical care, equal pay for equal work, open admissions for college, and many more. However, the degree of inequality persists with impoverished children and lack of care for the elderly and infirm. This persists in a nation which has the wealth to resolve many of these realities. It is at this point that the obligation of the truly wealthy becomes most apparent. If the wealthy were good stewards, they would strengthen the basic values of our democracy. Sadly, as individuals become extremely wealthy, their personal focus on the "eye of equality" is diminished.

If, however, a rich person commits to sharing his or her wealth extensively, beyond voluntary personal gifts, and share with the larger society without distinction of race, gender, or personal status, then that person becomes a good steward of democratic equality. To the degree that the wealthy do so, the country may go forward with affirming support for all who are gathered in democracy's house.

### *Sunday School and Our Democracy*

This single Bible story offers political guidance on the need to find a way for the wealthy to pass through the needle's eye of democracy and experience the redemptive power of positive citizenship we all owe for the privilege of living in this land. I could have learned even more in Sunday school from Bible stories that are filled with democratic values and the political obligations of citizenship. The story of Christ driving the money changers from the temple is a tale of ousting the wealthy from places where they may purchase political favor. And the story of Pharaoh's dreams of seven fat and seven lean cattle can be seen as a tale about careful resource management. Dominating many of these lessons is the absolute need for greater equity and fairness among all peoples, which we should adopt if the American experience in democratic values and practice is to survive well beyond our lifetimes.

As children, we ought to be immersed in our democratic faith by classes in social studies and civics. This training is not always done well. Too often, young people leave school without a clear understanding of how politics and government in America work. Once school is out, the details of our national faith may fade. We remember the guarantees of personal liberty while abandoning responsibility for defense of our democratic faith. It cannot be forgotten that our greatest obligation is to choose political action wisely, endorse equality, and abandon no one from the security that passage through the "needle's eye" provides.

# *Going to Vote*
## A Precious Responsibility

Election days meant that supper was going to be late. Election day was not a holiday and voters had to make time in their work day to get to the polls. Mom voted after she finished teaching for the day. Voting was a grown-up activity, but even as a small boy I got to participate! I got to stand with Mom in a line that moved slowly toward a table where each grown-up had to sign his or her name. After Mom wrote her name, a man handed her a ballot and we would stand in another line until one of the voting booths was empty. The voting booths were wooden frames with canvas hung on all sides. The canvas did not reach the floor and you could see the feet of other voters. The act of voting did not take a long. Mom would take the pencil that was attached to a string and make her choices. Then the really exciting event of the day happened. Mom would hand me her ballot and I got to put it in the ballot box!

After voting, it was back to the house to get supper ready. We would not eat until Dad returned from voting. He usually got home around seven o'clock and then would drive to the voting station. I did not get to go a second time because there were lots of people waiting to vote at the end of the day and lines could be long. Eventually, Dad would return and it would finally be time to eat. Our house had carried out its basic responsibility. The votes were cast. In our little space in democracy's house, citizenship was alive and well.

Voting is the most basic task of active citizenship; a simple act of waiting in line to fill out a ballot and express a preference. It affirms a belief in the democracy as your choice is recorded. Unfortunately, too many eligible American voters let election days go by without making their way to the polls. My mom and dad always voted. However, neither of them was busily engaged in political life. No bumper stickers on the Buick. No signs in the front yard. No going to political meetings, and I'm pretty sure there were no political donations. We, as a family, were quiet citizens who supported the war effort, flew the flag on all the holidays, went to the Memorial Day and 4th of July parades, and had quiet pride in being Americans. We kept our blackout curtains tightly closed at night during the war. And Mom and Dad voted in local elections, school board elections, congressional elections, and presidential elections.

### Voting and Equality in Our Democracy

In a system of government where wealthy people, like the symbolic freeholders of old, have great influence, preserving equality for all Americans requires participation by each citizen who is eligible to vote. Women and African-Americans, for whom the opportunity to vote was long denied, won their voting rights by courageous actions of individuals who demanded freedom and equality be extended to all citizens. The privilege of voting was achieved by personal valor and sacrifice. To fail to vote is to make American citizenship less meaningful and weaken the framework of our democracy. The ballot box is a means of ensuring greater equality by enabling citizens to choose the leaders who will uphold our basic beliefs. To not vote or to believe voting is unimportant is unpatriotic. When our political lives include voting regularly, the nation is stronger by the simple act of stepping into a voting booth at every opportunity.

## *As American as Apple Pie*

Reluctance to support the democratic process is well understood by people of power and influence who seek to control the outcome of elections. Our history is filled with strategies and schemes designed to discourage and prevent people from voting. Searching for ways to manipulate electoral outcomes is truly "as American as apple pie!" From the founding of the republic, when voting was denied to those without sufficient wealth, freedom and equality were limited. Later, as the country's population rapidly expanded and voting rights were extended without requiring wealth, the people in power needed new means of controlling election results. Election districts were designed to favor particular groups and reduce the influence of challengers. "Gerrymandering" became a well-understood strategy to influence election outcomes. More squalid techniques, including bribery, violence, and fraud, were commonplace.

The emancipation of slaves, the defeat of the southern states in the Civil War, and the passage of the 13th, 14th, and 15th Amendments to the Constitution produced a whole new set of strategies for suppressing the vote. The imposition of poll taxes, literacy tests, and Jim Crow laws across the American South provided evidence of how African-American citizens were effectively denied the rights of citizenship. A full century would pass before Congress affirmed voting rights for all Americans in the 1964 Voting Rights Act and created conditions to expand voter registration for generations of Americans long denied this privilege. Finally, it was not until 1920 before the nation resolved one of the great injustices of our land as the 19th Amendment granted women the right to vote after a persistent campaign of suffragettes that had lasted more than eighty years.

### *Voting Rights and Political Cowardice*

The attitudes toward voting rights held by colonial freeholders still persist among the people of privilege and wealth. And they are often not as certain of controlling outcomes as they would like to be. Consequently, the wealthy who are legally entitled to donate as much as they desire can invest large sums of money, which can change election results as media messages influence how people vote. But, it is apparent that spending vast amounts of money to support candidates and issues or do "negative" advertising about opponents is not sufficient for some of those descendants of the freeholders. They feel a need to be even more confident in getting the outcomes they desire.

In today's political climate, the desire to make voting more difficult has grown stronger. At the state and local levels, freeholders and other county government officials can have success in controlling the process of voting by limiting the number of days when voting may occur, imposing troublesome voter identification requirements, locating polling places in inconvenient places, reducing the number of places to vote, and challenging citizen groups who seek to enroll new voters. Some of these practices have been reversed by the courts. However, the intensity of the efforts to preserve dominance among people of wealth and influence in our political life indicates the consequences of inaction if the right to vote is not defended everywhere.

In a country that celebrates equality and freedom of choice, people who actively seek to suppress the vote are political cowards. They fear their ideas and candidates might not attract the support of the majority of voters. They know they risk failure in open debate in the marketplace of ideas. Therefore, they are so determined to achieve results for their candidates or their ideas, they seek to impose rules that contradict the basic principles of our democracy. Fearing defeat, they engage in repugnant political cowardice. The right to vote is as close to something sacred in a democracy as any element of our national life. It is the badge of citizenship for which many have suffered and indeed died. And still there are citizens of questionable intent or purpose who would deny those rights by cowardly maneuver and twisted behavior in pursuit of narrow political goals. Those who would seek to suppress the vote are in no manner patriots in America.

### *Voting to Redress Democracy's Imbalances*

Our system so historically tilted toward the influence of wealth on the political process has not changed. Indeed, it worsens as the gap between the exceptionally wealthy and the rest of society grows wider. The eye of equality in democracy's needle is an ever-present reality, measuring how the wealthy too often remain beyond the obligations that would ensure the promise of equality to all citizens. Wealth can equal influence, and influence can be used to control the outcomes of elections and the work done in the halls of government. To bring a better balance between influential wealth and the needs of the majority requires constant patriotic vigilance against cowardly practices so that no individual or group of individuals can deprive other citizens of the legitimate right to cast a ballot for the candidates of his or her choice or for referendums on how the government should act. Voting is a right that should not be denied.

# The "A" and "B" Stickers
## Education in the National Interest

During the war, our family car was a 1928 Buick. Mom used it every day to drive to the Willis School where she taught kindergarten. As a small boy, the distance from home to the school seemed a long way. It was probably less than ten miles, but driving at least a hundred miles each week for work when gasoline was rationed was a challenge.

To control the amount of gasoline a car owner could buy each month there were "ration stamps" that were symbolized by a sticker on the car's windshield. Nearly every car had an "A" sticker on the lower right corner of the windshield. The "A" indicated the car was using gasoline for domestic purposes. Our car was different. It had two stickers, an "A" and a "B." The "B" sticker indicated my family was entitled to have additional ration stamps and more gasoline. For my mom, it was also evidence of the importance the nation placed on the work she did. It was acknowledgment that teaching was critical to the national interest.

Education in time of war had a status that affirmed America's dedication to the importance of an educated people as a foundation of a vibrant democracy. Teaching five-year-olds at the Willis School in South Plainfield, New Jersey, was part of the war effort taking place in classrooms across the country. In the midst of global conflict in Europe and the Pacific, our country did not lose sight of the role that education plays in keeping the nation strong.

After the war, the "A" and "B" stickers were still on the windshield when the Buick was sold. Nevertheless, America remained committed to the importance of strong educational programs where young men and women could get the skills needed for a lifetime of work. One of the single greatest legislative actions for building the strength of our national workforce was a section of the "G.I. Bill" that allowed veterans to attend college at nominal cost. It shaped opportunities for millions to enter the middle class. Colleges and universities were thronged with men and some women who had fought valiantly and were committed to learning with the same dedication they had brought to military service.

That commitment to education was reaffirmed in the early years of my college education in 1957. We were all aware of the Cold War, which involved the potential use of nuclear weapons. But it came as a shock when the Russians put a rocket into orbit around the globe and demonstrated to the entire world that Soviet science was highly advanced and Russian school children could not only read but also do chemistry, physics, and engineering.

This startling reality caused a reaction in Washington that resulted in dramatic increases in federal support to education and rapid expansion of graduate programs to create the workforce of the post-industrial age, the workforce of technology and digital engineering. Similar to the examples of special ration stickers for jobs in the national interest, such as teaching, and low-cost college educations for returning troops, this new priority also linked education with the national interest. The federal legislation was called the N.D.E.A. – the National Defense Education Act.

Over time, the Soviet technological threat receded and America made great strides in space engineering by fulfilling President

Kennedy's goal of putting a man on the moon and returning him safely to earth by the end of the 60's. However, N.D.E.A. funding began to decline at the end of the 60's as resources that had previously supported education were diverted to the Vietnam war. Throughout this period of dramatic growth in university education there was not an equal commitment to elementary and secondary education, which was primarily funded at the state and local community levels. Rapid increases in the numbers of school-age populations stretched budgets. Moreover, schools were asked to take over parenting roles previously done in the home, including free breakfast and lunch, remedial work when students could not learn in the home, medical and counseling aid, options for dealing with teen pregnancy, and guidance for post-high school life in the basic tasks of entering the workplace. The learning that young men and women would need to go on to college was not sufficiently provided and colleges saw the growth of remedial learning programs. The link between supporting superior school systems and how that education would keep the nation strong and competitive was less apparent.

Going to college became popularly assumed to be a social right among a majority of young people. It was not tightly linked to national needs for the future. As long as the economy remained strong, the money spent on education remained sufficiently plentiful in most places to provide adequate, but not necessarily excellent, programs. And in less affluent communities that needed strong programs if young people were to have a chance to excel, financial resources were too often lacking. The civil rights era brought school desegregation and helped many more young people have access to a college education, but it also demonstrated how education was closely tied to social policy. Less attention was paid to national security policy and the economic and diplomatic challenges of foreign policy required to keep America safe and secure.

When economic downturns occur, education feels the pinch. Controlled at the state level with assistance from the national government, each state assesses priorities. Because school budgets are voted on separately from general operating budgets in most communities, the schools remain an easy target when it is believed cuts need to be made. Their budgets continue to be an annual opportunity for the public to express dismay with the leadership in communities, towns, and cities. However, their displeasure is misplaced as education suffers.

Unfortunately, we Americans tend to think too much in local terms. We remain unaware of what is happening around the globe where across Europe, Asia, South Asia, and Africa young people vigorously devote themselves to study and learning. In the twenty-first century, America has been distracted by lengthy wars and does not see how the rest of the world kept its focus on education as a fundamental ingredient to national progress. Only in recent years have we become more aware of our diminished competitive edge. There is need for drastic steps to increase students' performance levels, improve teacher training and standards, and improve our educational system as a whole.

## Losing the International STEM War

It would be fair to say that American life is being adversely influenced by the rise of industrial giants in Asia, South Asia, South America, and increasingly in sub-Saharan Africa. We have entered a time of true competitive economic warfare. Most countries in those parts of the world are dedicated to national goals of training their people to be more productive. Americans may lament the cuts to education budgets and our decreasing global rankings in key subjects, but neither Americans nor our leadership have yet to demand that educational performance in every state and community be defined as a critical variable in maintaining national competitiveness in the world economy and our strength as a super power.

Today there are few symbolic images of respect for teachers similar to the old "B" stickers on windshields of teachers' cars. Teachers' salaries are not calculated on the basis of "service in the national interest." The teaching profession today is not perceived to be as important as it was during the forty-five months from December of 1941 to August of 1945. Without professional recognition, increased levels of compensation, and provision of critical support in terms of equipment and instructional supplies, too many teachers leave the profession in less than five years. They are like soldiers who choose not to "re-up" for another tour.

For America to recapture and enhance its competitive advantage in science and math when compared to other countries, it must embark on a "STEM War" – a "Science, Technology, Engineering, and Math War" – which demands a commitment of economic resources far greater than all the costs required to win victory in World War II.

One way *not* to fight a STEM war is to demobilize our troops. Some estimates suggest more than 300,000 teachers lost their jobs in the first decade of the twenty-first century. No military commander wins a war by decommissioning more than *fifteen divisions* of the army. Consider the questionable logic of decimating your armies with lay-offs or demobilization and then lamenting the fact that the battle is being lost! You cannot win the war if you do not have the troops and the equipment to support them.

A STEM competition or "war" requires a return of tens of thousands of dedicated, well trained "boots on the ground" in better equipped classrooms all across the land. Every person who trains as a teacher and is certified by a state earns a commission in the Education War. The non-commissioned officers are the student interns being trained to be teachers and the teacher aides. As trained teachers advance in rank they should be acknowledged and paid at levels comparative to other professionals in commerce and industry. Their stature should be widely celebrated with medals and decorations acknowledging their effort to help win the Education War. Ensuring the battles occurring in every classroom and laboratory are successful requires adopting the best methods of teaching and training being utilized around the globe and providing the support funding that any army needs.

What is needed in America is a "National Defense Education Act, Part II" for our times.

It would demand massive expenditure to put education on a "war footing." We could all contribute. There ought to be "Education War Bonds" that even elementary school children could buy with weekly contributions of dollars and quarters, in the same way my brother and I and all my classmates brought our nickels and dimes to school each week to buy war bonds in the gloomy days after Pearl Harbor.

### *Looking Back, Looking Forward*

It is clear to me my mom was a soldier, a part of a great domestic army of "educational boots on the ground," defending the values that affirmed America as a great land. She and thousands of teachers like her taught the children of the Greatest Generation and then the Baby Boomers, preparing them for the advanced learning needed when America discovered the Russians had become highly skilled at science. For a teacher during the war years of the early 1940's, a "B" sticker on the windshield in war time was as good as a campaign ribbon. For teachers in the Education War, there should be status and compensation to attract the brightest minds and young men and women who will willingly "re-up" for multiple tours of duty in our schools. What is required is an enlarged sense of patriotic duty on behalf of world class learning, realignment of wealth to support the education war effort, and equal access to the voting booth to support the issues that will produce the educated citizenry required to achieve educational goals, just as the nation once achieved military victory three quarters of a century ago. Unstinting support for education is a vital political virtue for everyone living in Democracy's house!

# Part Three:

# Political People

# *FDR Has Died:*
## Who Can Be a Great Leader?

It was late afternoon on an overcast April day in 1945 when Georgie Christianson, the big kid who lived next door, came out his back door and walked over to the fence between our houses and said, "Did you hear the news? The President is dead!" Georgie was in high school. He never talked to me or seemed to know I existed. But he must have needed to talk to someone. I had not heard the news. The radios at our house were only turned to kids' shows in the late afternoon or in the early morning to a small radio in the bathroom that Dad listened to while he shaved. As to the president, I may have been vaguely aware we had someone in charge of America, but I had no idea what he did. I may also have heard the name Roosevelt.

In our house, the subject of politics did not come up. I'm sure that dad never voted for a Democrat, and we never talked about the presidential elections in '48, '52, or '56. I can only assume that Dad was unhappy when Truman won in '48 but content with the two Eisenhower victories. Mom was always quiet about her choices and waited until 1969 to tell Dad she had voted for Kennedy. I also remember arriving home from university for Thanksgiving in 1960. Dad picked me up at the bus station. As we drove down our street, he caught sight of a neighbor's car pulling into its driveway. It had a Kennedy sticker on the bumper. Dad's reaction was, "Well I'll be darned! Walt Keim voted for Kennedy and he's not a Catholic!" After a few seconds, I quietly said, "Dad, a lot of us did!" Then there was silence that stretched through the entire weekend. By Christmas he was in a better mood as Kennedy appointed some Presbyterians to his cabinet.

That was how political talk did not occur in our house. It just did not come up at the dinner table, and I cannot remember any political discussions when the aunts, uncles, and cousins gathered for family picnics or on holidays. There might have been complaints about "That damn man in the White House!" being re-elected to a fourth term, but in 1945 it was hard to be negative about a president who was on the verge of winning the war in Europe and gradually tightening the military noose around Japan in the Pacific.

Hearing that President Roosevelt had died was just a fact to puzzle over. FDR was the only person who had ever been president in my lifetime and, apparently, had been president for a very long time. Since I was going to be seven on my next birthday the death of FDR found a place in the early pages of my political memory. I do remember that after FDR died there was talk about whether Vice President Harry Truman was up to the job. I think all of the country was probably surprised by how strong Truman proved to be in his first days in office. After less than four months, he made the decision to use atomic bombs on Hiroshima and Nagasaki, avoiding a military invasion of Japan and saving thousands of soldiers' lives. I also remember what happened right after the bombs were dropped. On August 15, 1945 my family was returning from a few days of holiday at Asbury Park on the Jersey shore. We drove home in the falling darkness of a late summer evening. As the old Buick passed through Englishtown all the sirens went off. Dad pulled over to find out what was the matter. A man said, "The war's over! The Japs surrendered!"

In the following months I accumulated political memories at a faster rate. The radio reported on the newly created United Nations. Right after the war there were lots of stories about the troops coming home from Europe. Tom Howell, a Navy commander, arrived home to his parent's house across the street and Bobby Thompson who lived four houses away came home in his sparkling whites from service in the navy. The Memorial Day and July 4th parades had lots of veterans in uniform and rank upon rank of "Gold Star Mothers" in their white dresses striding by in formation; every step a reminder that each of them had sent a son off to battle and would never see them come home.

What became clear to me as an elementary school student passing from the first to the sixth grade was that Truman was very different from Roosevelt. However, both men were given the same powers of the presidency and both used that power to win a war, make important decisions about the peace, and stand up to the formidable threats of the Nazis and then the Communists. In school, we became aware of the Communist victory in China and the rise to power of a man named Mao. The *Saturday Evening Post* and *Colliers* carried frightening stories about the Russians with illustrations that could worry the imagination of even a small boy.

The lesson gained from all of this was that our president was vitally important and the kind of person who sat in the White House mattered. The differences between FDR and Harry Truman also taught us that we cannot know how well someone will lead until they are in the office. No matter how qualified someone seems for the job, presidential performance is only truly revealed once a president is in the job and making decisions about how the country will be governed and protected from enemies overseas.

### *Origins of Politicians*

The personalities of presidents are critical in determining how America is governed. It is our responsibility as citizens to learn as much as possible about the character of presidential candidates. Examination must be made into how a candidate sees the world, his or her sense of obligation to the less fortunate, and commitment to the values of equality, fairness, and freedom for all Americans. It is useful to know if they did well in school and how childhood friends remember them. Were they well-liked? Did they ever have a minimum wage job or do manual labor? What have been the disappointments in their lives? How did they overcome setbacks and learn from mistakes? No candidate is perfect, but by the time he or she is being considered for the most important job in America, his or her character, values, and behavior are vital information. Understanding the importance of presidential character has occurred over seven decades as I have watched nearly a dozen men serve in that office. Each was notably unique. Some displayed great skills and leadership. Others were more reluctant to use the office as effectively as possible.

Presidents' characters shape our country's fortunes. They influence national prosperity or economic downturns. People's lives can be hurt by presidential choices. Those choices must consider all Americans rather than a select few. It is not true that the government is so vast and complex that one person cannot make a big difference. Indeed, a president can make a great deal of difference. When we vote for a presidential candidate we should ask ourselves, "What was he or she like growing up? How has he or she helped others who were less fortunate? Will he or she be dedicated to protecting those who cannot protect themselves?" If you can find positive answers to those three questions, then you will probably make a reasonable choice.

### Hot Houses of Ambition

Historically, there are some common characteristics of politicians who choose to be fully engaged in public life. Politicians tend to come from middle-class homes that have been labelled "hot houses" of ambition. In those homes, they were encouraged to take advantage of every opportunity to do well. They are likely to have had parents, especially mothers, who praised their achievements and insisted on discipline that kept them working hard. Children who wanted affection knew better than to disappoint their parents.

Why are middle class homes important? They are places where there is good reason to positively believe success is possible if a child is strongly encouraged to succeed. By contrast, in homes with very limited resources parents and children may have less hope for the future and are discouraged enough to believe there is limited hope of success no matter how hard a child works. In the homes of the rich a child may be less determined to work diligently because he or she already has abundant advantages. These differences between the various economic levels in American society support the idea of middle-class youth being most motivated for success. Indeed, a significant portion of political leaders will emerge from these households. These children are challenged to excel and gain recognition by meeting parental standards for excellence in school work, sports, or other youthful activities.

Another important variable to consider as a motivator of future politicians is how their lives were lived in the family home. Young people who later become politicians tend to work hard to earn the love and affection of their parents. If love and affection is not returned even when performance on school work or other activities is outstanding, the child can resent such a lack of appreciation. That withholding of parental affection can have an effect years later when politicians compensate for lack of love in the family by searching for public recognition to offset the earlier disappointments in the home.

Consider successful presidential candidates of the past eight decades. Many fit this profile as they sought to excel from middle-class beginnings. Eisenhower graduated from West Point, Nixon left California to attend Duke Law School, Johnson came from a poor background in west Texas and trained as a teacher, Humphrey worked in a soda shop before attending university and becoming a lawyer. McGovern came out of South Dakota and trained as a lawyer. Jimmy Carter grew up on a peanut farm but went to the Naval Academy. Reagan started early with a career in broadcasting that led to success in Hollywood. Bill Clinton excelled in high school in Hope, Arkansas, before going to Georgetown University and Yale. Obama grew up in Hawaii and Indonesia with a single parent, his mom, before attending college in California, graduating from Columbia University, and going on to Harvard Law School. In each case, the family histories of presidential candidates are important in understanding the forces that drove them to succeed.

Of course, there are exceptions to this profile. However, the number of wealthy men who succeeded to the highest office in the twentieth century is small. The Roosevelts, Teddy, and Franklin are examples. The same is true of Kennedy and the Bushes. However, these examples of affluent men achieving the oval office are fewer than those who began life in middle-class homes. Furthermore, these special five presidents came from households where public service was a basic tenant of family life.

The backgrounds of the current generation of political leaders is vitally important as these men and women make decisions to seek public acclaim for reasons buried in their childhoods. It is likely there are dozens of congressmen, congresswomen and governors who are tempted to imagine themselves as candidates for the country's highest office. Indeed, a few of them may even carry a rough draft of their nomination acceptance speech in their back pockets.

Studies of political origins and character indicate politicians do not "accidentally" arrive on the public stage. They tend to come from backgrounds that include a desire to rise to public prominence, connected to experiences growing up. They pursue a commitment to public service for which we can be grateful, but they may very well be driven by personal motivations to seek the limelight. Knowing backgrounds can be a key as to how they will perform responsible roles of governing.

### *Politicians and Democracy*

I was not cognizant of the need to discover all these facts about presidents on that rainy April day in 1945. I was barely aware of such an important event in American history and the national concern as to how Truman, a less-than-successful clothing store owner who had never seemed to be presidential material, would handle leading our country. We were to learn of his compassion for all Americans as he integrated the armed forces. We were to witness his important decisions to save Europe from Communist control, ensure the establishment of the UN, and celebrate the peace by creating new opportunities for the hundreds of thousands of returning warriors and citizen patriots who served overseas or here at home building the "arsenal of democracy" that won the war. In a world that grows ever more complex and potentially dangerous from military accidents or mistakes knowing the character of the man or woman who is elected to the presidency is of absolute importance.

## *The Wild West*
### A Fading Frontier in American Politics

My childhood toys were made of sturdy stuff: wood, metal, and cast iron. The ones that provided hours of creative activity were American Bricks, Lincoln Logs, Lionel trains, and Erector sets. American Bricks, the Legos of that age, were made of wood and snapped together to build sturdy little houses. It was important to never let them get wet because the wood would expand and they would no longer fit together. Legos are much better. Lionel trains and erector sets were my brother's fascination. For me, Lincoln Logs were the best. My collection grew as I received new boxes of wooden logs on birthdays and Christmases. The logs eventually filled a large wooden crate, with room for dozens of toy soldiers, cowboys, and Indians. Rainy days were spent building forts, cabins, and redoubts for battles between attacking Indians and defending soldiers and cowboys.

Those boyhood creations gave shape to my romantic notions of the American West that were so much a part of my childhood. Books, newspaper comics, and movies made tales of the American frontier seem real. The kids in the neighborhood loved the Saturday morning movies at the Liberty Theater. For twenty-five cents we could see a cowboy double feature with Tom Mix, Roy Rogers, Gene Autry, or "Hopalong" Cassidy, plus lots of Bugs Bunny cartoons and the Warner-Pathe "News of the World." One glorious day, I had a lucky number on my ticket and won a pair of Acme cowboy boots. They were so special I was even allowed to wear them to church. Sadly, my feet grew too fast and within a year the boots no longer fit.

As my reading skills improved, I anxiously awaited the arrival of Red Ryder comic books in the mail. Western stories were serialized in the Saturday Evening Post. On the radio, there was the weekly broadcast of the Lone Ranger to go along with Lone Ranger comic books. All that material was the background for endless games of "cowboys and Indians" played in the woods behind the houses on both sides of Catalpa Avenue. You had to have a cap pistol that looked like a cowboy's gun and a holster. The most realistic cap pistols were the long-barreled ones with a revolving chamber that required a reload after six shots.

These images of the American West were shaped by what I read, saw in movies, built with Lincoln Logs, and played in childhood games. The New Jersey suburbs allowed for youthful imagination of the American West as a place of heroic adventures by brave pioneers. It was far from the rugged reality of the life that had existed on the American frontier and the history of native American Indians that, like African-American history, was not taught to us in school or presented in print or on the radio.

In school, the heroism of the American frontier was reinforced by our social studies education. We learned early about Abe Lincoln, the rail splitter, who did his homework by drawing on the back of a shovel with only a piece of charcoal in the light from the fireplace. We saw romantic pictures of wagon trains carrying settlers West and heard stories of the hardships and sacrifices by men and women who went out to the Oregon territory. We learned of the bravery and courage of individual frontiersmen.

Daniel Boone's exploits moved from the pages of our books to the TV screen in the 1950's. In story and song, we were told of Andrew Jackson's victory over the British in the Battle of New Orleans and of the many brave souls, including Davey Crockett, who died heroically at the Battle of the Alamo. We learned about homesteaders who built sod houses, plowed the Great Plains, and settled the West beyond the Mississippi. The tales of the Pony Express were exciting to read and visualize. We marveled at the effort to build the Transcontinental Railway with celebration of its completion by the driving of the golden spike at Promontory Point in Utah. It was a romantic but distorted view of the West, but it was the image held by easterners who had never visited the American West.

From the perspective of later years, it is unfortunate that as children we did not learn about the manner in which American Indians were mistreated by the government and by many of the people who went to the West as settlers. Only in the last half of the twentieth century were Americans made more fully aware of the way in which the culture of American Indians was ignored and hidden from the history lessons in schools and in popular understanding of the West.

### *Politicians and the Log Cabin Myth*

The history and romance of the American frontier was more than childhood fantasy. The story of the West produced a large amount of scholarship that examines how our American democracy was shaped by the frontier experience. The most prominent scholarship on the frontier was written by historian Frederick Jackson Turner. The Frontier Thesis or "Turner Thesis" argues American democracy was shaped from the conditions of the American frontier. Turner even determined the frontier closed in the 1890's, when the last land available for homesteading was settled. There is useful reality here as we know how immigrants came from Europe, went west and built homes, towns, and eventually cities with little or no knowledge about democracy. They learned to govern themselves. They built communities, figured out how to govern, implemented laws, and made those experiences into histories of life on the frontier. Of course, all the rules about how politics functions were played out there and when populations grew large enough to result in statehood, the representatives sent east to serve in the Congress brought with them a view of political life that had been created in the great American West.

It is reasonable to accept the history of a frontier that had real influence American politics. In the 1830's, a candidate with extensive frontier experience made his way to the Oval Office. Andrew Jackson ended the reign of presidents from the Virginian aristocracy and the Adam's family of New England who dominated the first fifty years of American independence. Jackson's presidency began a period when presidents came from states more inland than the original thirteen colonies, had extensive military experience on the frontier, or both. Except for Jackson's successor, Martin Van Buren, and later Millard Fillmore, the frontiersman/soldier image fits all our presidents in the nineteenth century. Some were born on the rural frontier and nearly all had military appointments that included service in the Mexican-American War and the Civil War.

The trust invested in men with backgrounds developed on the edges of a rapidly growing country became the basis of the "log cabin" theory of American politics by which it was believed to be an asset for presidential candidates to have lived at least part of their lives in harsh frontier conditions or to have served in uniform which in the nineteenth century meant the West until the start of the Civil War. As the West was settled by the end of the 1800's, the profile of the soldier leader continued in politics, remaining so strong that in the twentieth century all but five of our presidents came from rural or small-town beginnings and many had various forms of military service. Except for the aforementioned five eastern presidents from wealthy backgrounds, the "log cabin" theory about rural birthplaces of presidents was preserved.

The pattern of presidents from rural backgrounds has been so consistent that it seems extraordinary. We ought to ask why we did not have more presidents who were born in New York, Boston, Philadelphia or Charleston. Rural Ohio of the nineteenth century produced more presidents than any other state. More basically, what is it about life in the rural areas and small towns of America that has made young men dream of being President? It is a common feature in the lives of William McKinley of Niles, Ohio; Woodrow Wilson born in rural Virginia; Warren Harding of Corsica, Ohio; Calvin Coolidge of Plymouth Notch, Vermont; Harry Truman of Lamar, Missouri; Dwight Eisenhower of Denison, Texas; Richard Nixon from tiny Yorba Linda, California; Gerald Ford born in Omaha; Jimmy Carter of Plains, Georgia; Ronald Reagan of Tampico, Illinois; and Bill Clinton of Hope, Arkansas. Clearly, most of our presidents have come from notably rural places

### *Wanting to Be Somebody!*

Research into the kinds of households from which politicians emerge suggests it is not merely the Frontier Thesis that explains how birth in rural environments encouraged a desire to fill prominent political roles. Rather, a simpler theory was proposed by the political scientist Harold Lasswell who suggested these were people who wanted to succeed more than people from cities or emerging metropolitan areas. People raised in rural areas or small towns wanted to get away from places offering little opportunity. Looking at their histories, you can see that early determination. Our presidents have often abandoned rural environments to become teachers, engineers, military officers, lawyers, radio personalities, actors and businessmen before becoming President.

The time may have now arrived when a rural farmer is rarely nominated for the presidency, but the conditions that encourage a young man or woman to escape from any small town and dedicate their lives to "being somebody" important still prevail. Becoming president is not a likely goal in the early years of one's life, but setting out to acquire prominence is what leads to careers where a presidency becomes possible.

### *The Disappearance of the Romantic Frontier*

The development of the Frontier Thesis to explain the rugged growth of America's democratic institutions and the "log cabin" theory as a foundation for successful political lives is now fading away in the twenty-first century. Movies about the American West are fewer in number. The interests of young people have shifted to space odysseys, imagined worlds of myth, science fiction warfare, and a broader interest in the global environment. The fascination with the romanticized Old West has withered. And the arrival of millions of immigrants from all corners of the globe has further diminished the legends and legacies of America's frontier heritage.

As America assumed greater power status after World War II,

our attention shifted to foreign policy challenges, the winning of the Cold War, the prosecution of and eventual loss of a war in Southeast Asia, the collapse of the Soviet Union, the tragedy of 9/11, and the wars in Iraq and Afghanistan. The importance of this shift now affects our national political life and the apparent weakening of the "down-home" virtues of small town life. Concern for neighbors and a willingness to cooperate and listen seem increasingly lost in national politics. But even as the vestiges of frontier life become less visible, the importance of being successful in politics still carries an obligation to appear as a "regular guy or gal" no matter how much money as been accumulated.

## New Generations of Politicians

What will probably not change is the role of middle-class households. The great metropolitan areas may flourish and produce people with technological skills and global interests, but statistically, they may not necessarily have the same drive for political eminence that encourages young people from small towns and medium-sized cities. All these new generations, urban and rural, will be more digitally savvy and connected to the media, but the people from smaller communities may well have the greatest determination to succeed on bigger stages of national life.

## The Prairie Myth Fades Away

My Lincoln Logs and toy soldiers were sold in a garage sale when I realized my son was never going to play with such ancient toys. The buyer was younger than myself and seemed to be reliving a chapter from his own youth in his eagerness to have such a large trove of Lincoln Logs. What I remember most fondly, however, are all my days of childhood play that imagined life in frontier places while growing up in suburban New Jersey. However, my reality was a short train ride to the streets of New York City and visits to the Bronx Zoo, Radio City Music Hall, Ebbetts Field, the Polo Grounds, Yankee Stadium and Madison Square Garden. It was a childhood that did not encourage me to seek more exciting places than the house on Catalpa Avenue. That drive to succeed was left to young men growing up in places like Plains, Georgia; Tampico, Illinois; Yorba Linda, California; or Hope, Arkansas.

## *Suppertime*
### Discovering Political Realities

Suppertime was always a family affair. It did not start until Dad got home from work. His train got in at 6:45 and was followed by a twenty-minute walk from the station. Mom usually arrived home from teaching a little after five. Supper was ready when Dad came through the front door. When we were small, there were six of us around the table, including Mom's Great Aunt. Dad would say grace and dish up each plate. It was a ritual for every weekday evening throughout my childhood. Saturdays brought an earlier supper time since Mom and Dad did not work on weekends. On Sundays, the biggest meal of the day was right after church, and suppers were more informal gatherings around the kitchen table. Sundays meant popovers, pancakes or waffles with the radio shows Amos 'N' Andy and Jack Benny in the background.

### *"Come and Sit Down, Supper is Ready!"*

Dinner time conversation was usually about what happened in our school or Mom's school day. Dad rarely talked about work at the Empire Trust Company, but he sometimes mentioned something interesting he had seen on the train to Hoboken or the ferry ride over to lower Manhattan. We did not talk about sports. We did talk about the neighborhood, the new houses going up, and new neighbors moving to Catalpa Avenue and surrounding streets. The main topic was usually about life at school, our teachers, what happened on the playground, and the weekly assemblies where we saw movies or had guest speakers. We talked about classmates and described any time someone new joined our class. My class consisted of the same bunch of kids who moved through the grades together. The two dozen kids in my kindergarten class all graduated from high school together. And, of course, we also talked a lot about what we were reading and learning.

It was the descriptions of our school work that could get Dad talking. His favorite topic was American history, especially Civil War history, about which he knew a great deal. He would tell us about his Great Uncle John who lived on the family farm and told stories of life as a soldier in the Civil War, including being wounded by a musket ball in his rear end! And if my brother, sister, or I were memorizing a poem for school, Dad could really get going and recite long passages of poetry. This always seemed amazing to us as we struggled to memorize Poe's "The Raven" or lines from "Snowbound," while Dad held all those lines perfectly in his mind more than thirty years after learning them!

Those dinner table conversations were also important as they influenced the type of lives we would lead. At the dinner table, we decided we would be teachers. From the time she was six, my sister told everyone that she wanted to be a teacher, like Mom. She never wavered from that goal and eventually taught kindergarten. I was fascinated by American history and decided early on that I wanted to teach history in a high school. My older brother Dave was less outgoing; he told fewer stories at dinner and shared less about his ambitions for the future, but he was the hardest working of the three of us and the most able student. Once he was in high school, he grew more committed to math and science and decided to be an engineer. His days as a teacher would wait until he retired from a career in research that produced a fistful of patents at the Johns-Manville Corporation. My sister taught for four decades, excluding some time off when her children were small. I taught for forty years, but never in a high school.

## Suppertime in the Neighborhood

In all our suppertime conversations, I never gave any thought to the conversations happening at the evening meals of all my classmates. What did they talk about? Our family dinner times were probably a bit different because both Mom and Dad worked. Most of the kids I went to school with only had fathers who worked outside the house. In my classes at the West End School, I was the only kid who brought a lunch box; everyone else went home for lunch. This meant we heard information about Dad's work in New York and Mom's stories of what was happening in her classroom. And those conversations at dinner helped shape our choices of what we wanted to be.

I knew a little bit about what other kids' fathers did. David Harris' dad was our school principal. Bobby Bennett's dad was a cop. Lois Feller's father and her uncle owned a fuel company, and Barry Rosenbaum's father and uncles owned Rosenbaums' Department Store. Other kids' fathers in my neighborhood worked in the big Mack Truck plant, owned restaurants, or were bankers, city employees, or shop owners. In an age when television had yet to become popular, our news came from the radio, newspapers, and what parents brought home and shared at the dinner table. Fathers who were lawyers, bankers, or in commercial business could talk about the economy or laws affecting their professions. Pastors, social service professionals, or doctors probably shared totally different subjects. All those conversations helped decide my classmates' futures.

At least a clue about the different kinds of dinner conversations was unearthed by going through old high school yearbooks and looking at the "future plans" of my classmates. The majority did not plan to enroll in the classic four-year college degree programs. Most girls were thinking about jobs in store sales or secretarial positions, and a few considered becoming teachers. The majority of the boys were planning on enlisting in the armed forces or just getting a job. At the Thanksgiving Day high school football game after graduating from high school there was a chance to see old classmates. Many of the boys were planning to drop out of college after just one semester. Most of the girls were already working or in training for jobs. It was the 50's, and the explosion in higher education brought about by the G.I. Bill had yet to be fully absorbed. "Going to college" was still in transition, but within a decade kids realized that college was becoming a necessity for getting ahead in the world.

### *Influence on Careers in Public Service*

The third piece of the framework for examining the influences that encourage people to choose lives in the public eye is the importance of family conversations. The studies by Harold Lasswell concluded that, one, middle-class homes were "hot houses" of ambition, two, rural or suburban towns produced the most driven politicians and, three, the importance of family conversations, were a stimulus to considering a life in politics. In that pre-television age, choices and dreams were formed around dining tables. It is reasonable to assume that the dinner table was where children first heard talk of school budgets, zoning ordinances, business growth, local elections, and national elections. They began to absorb the excitement of careers in public life.

Political opinions formed in childhood tend to remain unchanged until late adolescence. When registering to vote, teenagers usually choose the party of their parents. However, a change is possible as adolescence turns to adulthood. Being away from home at college or moving into a career may cause a rethinking of political opinions. A progressive may become more conservative or vice versa. However, if political opinions do not shift in late adolescence, then political preferences tend to persist throughout adulthood. Not surprisingly, the children of families where historic attitudes about privilege for the wealthy continue to flourish will likely continue to hold those views. Homes which endorse the importance of governmental responsibility to protect all members of society are more likely to have children who favor progressive political interests.

### *Politics and Dinner Table Talk*

It can be hoped that suppertime in America will continue to remain important in shaping lives, dreams, goals, and personal commitments. The distractions of the digital age and the diverse daily routines of family members can impose a burden on families trying to routinely gather together each evening. The lessons learned and values absorbed at our dinner table are not easily convertible to Instagram, numbered character texts, or brief emails. If we are to understand politics and politicians, we need those lessons of civics once taught across the dinner table, for our own sake and for all Americans in democracy's house. Having supper as a family is a tradition worth keeping.

## *Buying the Britannica*
### Sources of Political Strength

When I was seven, my parents made an important investment for the futures of my brother, my sister, and me. It was such a big decision that even as kids we sensed the cost would strain carefully balanced family finances. The choice to make the big purchase began one evening when a man came to the house to show Mom and Dad some beautifully bound books with gold lettering. They looked over the contents and asked lots of questions before the samples were packed up and the man went away. Then there was more discussion. Days passed before mother finally announced we would be getting a full set of the *Encyclopedia Britannica*. Then she explained what an encyclopedia was. As children, we knew this was something special, very expensive, and bought for use in our school work.

More time passed before a truck delivered two wooden crates. Inside, the volumes were carefully packed and looked beautiful. One by one, each volume was placed in a glass-fronted case at the bottom of the stairs where you could not pass to the living room, dining room, or kitchen without seeing this impressive new addition to our house. The *Britannica* filled the entire top shelf and part of the bottom shelf of the cabinet. There was just enough room left on the bottom so that another encyclopedia could be added later – the *World Book*. Together, this collection of knowledge was the core of the family library while we were in school. We used the books constantly. They were our references for any facts we wanted to know. We followed the *World Book* motto: "We never guess, we look it up!" The *World Book* was easier to use, but when more detail was needed, the *Britannica* was the best place to find out "stuff." It was also the place where you learned things you were not looking to find. A page would get interesting, and soon you had read that page and the next page as well.

What my brother, sister and I failed to appreciate was how the *Britannica* purchase was a decision Mom and Dad made as an investment in the future of their children. They were quietly entertaining the hope their children might go to college. They were harboring a wish we might one day accomplish something they had not achieved: a baccalaureate degree. Without knowing how such lofty goals would be accomplished, my parents chose how the lives of children aged four, seven, and eleven would proceed. Our obligation was to measure up to our parents' aspirations for us.

Buying the *Britannica* was a symbol of commitment to education, the basic tool for getting ahead in America at a time when few Americans had college degrees. College was by no means a given. Dad's education after high school was a course at the Rider Business Institute in Princeton, and Mom's post-high school education was two years at Montclair Normal School for Teacher Training.

Everyone knows the advice to "Get a good education!" But in an era when America was recovering from the Depression and the dislocations of wartime with its rationing and shortages, young people did not fully appreciate the fact that the more education you had the more money you would earn. In the 1940's, only 6% of high schoolers went on to college. Most public schools had not yet developed systems for tracking student performance and separating young people into college prep versus general education tracks. Everyone took woodshop or home economics.

One thing is clear: my high school guidance counselor did more driver's education teaching than counseling. We students at North Plainfield High School were on our own to find out about colleges, especially if our parents had not gone on to any schooling when they finished high school. My parents were at least interested in college education without knowing what it was all about. In the end, I applied to Montclair State Teachers College and half a dozen small liberal arts colleges where I could study history and become a certified teacher. My sister Ellen, with lots of urging from Mom, was accepted at Wheelock College which specialized in training kindergarten teachers. Dave enrolled at Clarkson College of Technology to study engineering.

### *In Pursuit of the Things We Want*

The reason for going to college was not explained well. When we asked, we were told, "You'll get a better job!" or "You'll make more money!" The more important message we missed was that a good education was not an end in itself. It is only a beginning. Of what? Something not realized until we got older when becoming more fully aware of a bigger world beyond our neighborhood and our school. Eventually, we began to think like grown-ups and shaped images of having a good job, a nice house, good health, friends, and maybe even a loving family of our own. At some point, each of us formed our own personal wish lists.

To understand individual wish lists it is important to have an organized method. By doing this we can understand why some people focus on becoming politicians and desire to have positions where they can exercise power over others. A useful study by Harold Lasswell and Abraham Kaplan entitled *Power and Society* provides such a framework for looking at individual desires utilizing eight values or preferences. This framework leads to understanding how what we desire shapes our lives. The things we value most tend to determine what we do with our lives. The eight values or preferences used in the study are: "enlightenment," "skill," "wealth," "respect," "well-being," "rectitude," "affection," and "power."

All the value preferences are linked together. If you acquire one, it can help you acquire another. For example, a person who dreams of being a doctor knows he or she must acquire "skills" in medical training after first acquiring the "enlightenment" of a general college degree which is preparation for medical school. The order in which we acquire these preferences reveals a pattern describing how we build our lives and careers. By working hard in school, we gain "enlightenment" that precedes advanced study in certain professions. When the preferences of "enlightenment" and "skill" are combined, a person is prepared to enter a profession where he or she can acquire "wealth." Success in a career can bring recognition from the community in the form of "respect." And with the benefits of the combined values of "enlightenment", "skill", "wealth" and "respect", a person can acquire both physical and psychological "well-being." Someone with all these values would theoretically be healthy, happy, loved, and successful!

It is clear how one value/preference builds a foundation for acquiring other values/preferences that we desire. Notably, a person born into a wealthy family has a significant advantage as getting an education is less of a struggle and skill training after college is not a financial burden. However, a person born with very few resources can still acquire desired values by first getting a good education and thereafter acquire one preference after another as a career is built and success achieved.

There are also cases when other values/preferences shape our lives. A young man or woman with athletic talent, which is physical "well-being," can achieve triumphs in sports. For example, Cassius Clay's physical ability was the foundation for acquiring "skill" as a boxer and a gold medal at the 1960 Olympics. His success led to championships and great "wealth." Exceptional "skill" and "wealth" resulted in international "respect." Then Cassius Clay converted to Islam and changed his name to Mohammed Ali using his fame to take a stand against military service in what he considered an unjust war in Vietnam. He was celebrated worldwide for his conscientious commitment to his faith, acquiring not just "respect" but also moral "rectitude." His achievement did not necessarily grow from basic education, but along the way he acquired a broader view of the world, an "enlightened" view of humanity. Unfortunately, the punishment his body absorbed over so many years of fighting led to a decline in his health and may have contributed to the early onset of Parkinson's disease, which resulted in a loss of his once vibrant physical "well-being."

Another example tells a story of a young man who grew up in a religious home where his father was a preacher. The young man went to college for "enlightenment" and then chose to go to seminary and acquire the "skill" to serve as a minister. Following ordination, he returned home and became a central figure in the civil rights struggles in the 1960's. He gained significant influence among both the African-American and white communities in America which resulted in "respect," "rectitude," and a Nobel

Peace Prize. He never gained great "wealth," and was deprived of physical "well-being" when assassinated in 1968. The expressed sorrow of the nation and his family revealed a measure of "affection" our country held for Martin Luther King Jr. With the support of the *Britannica,* my brother, sister, and I gained adequate "enlightenment" in our house on Catalpa Avenue to pursue training in college and acquire the "skills" needed to pursue the careers we desired. Dave ultimately had his moments of satisfaction during his research in thermodynamics while working for the Johns-Manville Corporation. Ellen was a successful elementary school teacher for decades. I diverged from American history into international relations and African studies while in graduate school and worked at the university level for more than forty years while making more than two dozen trips to Africa. Along the way, we earned "respect" from colleagues, "affection" within our families, and personal "well-being" in our lives. We never became wealthy, but we lived in relative comfort.

### *Wealth, Power, and Politics*

The pursuit of "power" has the most impact on our understanding of politics. Many individuals may pursue "enlightenment" and "skills" to satisfy their interests as scholars, scientists, doctors, artists, athletes, and pastors. They do this to acquire a personal sense of "well-being," "respect," and even moral recognition or "rectitude" in the subjects and professions to which they are dedicated. Along the way, they may acquire sufficient "wealth" so that they can live comfortably, but the central purpose of their lives is their "skills," a broadening view of the world, and a commitment to larger goals of inquiry or service.

There are other individuals, however, who seek "skill" and "enlightenment" not as an end, but as a means for acquiring that which they most desire: "power." They combine the development of other values to advance careers that will eventually fulfill their desires to influence decisions, which is fundamental to holding a sense of power.

For those who are wealthy, the accumulation of more wealth beyond personal needs can aid their interests in acquiring other value preferences. Notably, most who achieve great wealth remain satisfied with their success and the "respect" such privilege provides. Their "wealth" may inspire philanthropy that can encourage high regard and even "rectitude," depending on the causes they choose to support. The wealthy can live in comfort and security that includes "affection" from those closest to them and contentment so they can resist temptations to acquire more "power" beyond the management of their fortunes.

It is apparent that contentment with "wealth" is not satisfactory to some portion of the wealthy who acquire the "power" to control political outcomes in their communities, states, and the nation. Their fortunes are a means to that end as they join other people who are singularly motivated to seek "power" but must do so without great wealth. But those less wealthy power-seekers usually have the skill to bring "wealth" from others to support their aims and are willing to use all their other resources of "skill," "enlightenment," "respect," "rectitude," "well-being," and "affection" to advance personal agendas for electoral triumph or public appointment.

The people who become power-pursuers are often inspired by the conversations around the dinner table that build dreams of great prominence. As they pursue their dreams, they practice skills that may suggest great love for their supporters, concern for citizens in general, and respect for those who can advance their careers. They are skillful in all the nuances of politics as they move upward to places of influence where they can have the satisfaction of controlling outcomes and hope to experience affection from the larger population.

Because striving for "power" is common to all who seek public prominence, it is absolutely vital to know the details of their lives. If they have fundamental beliefs in serving the needs of others and being of assistance to entire communities, then they may be judged as good stewards of public needs. If power-seekers fail to display characteristics of genuine concern for communities and those in need they must be judged as poor stewards of the public welfare and unsuited for public responsibility. It is fundamental that acquisition of skills and means for success in public life must be balanced by equally careful judgments as to the motivation of political power-seekers.

At the house on Catalpa Avenue, our attention was not focused on dreams of power. We were seeking knowledge based on the *World Book* motto, "We do not guess and look it up!" And we found out more stuff than we ever could have imagined. We used that learning to be admitted to colleges where we could train for specific futures and anticipate satisfying lives as adults. We did not contemplate becoming people seeking to influence the lives of others beyond classrooms where we taught and laboratories where we created new products. We kept to our own little space in democracy's house. In contrast, it was the future politicians who had experiences in their homes and careers of applying "enlightenment" and "skills" to be successful in ways that led to positions of influence over the making of consequential decisions.

Part Four

Political Practices

# *Harry and Ike*

## Parties, Politics, and Limited Opportunities

August of 1948 when I celebrated my tenth birthday was an election year in which Republicans sought to gain control the White House after sixteen years of Democratic rule. I was aware of this event but had little knowledge of how the process worked. That summer, all the talk was about party conventions to decide who would be the candidates. The Republicans believed Mr. Dewey deserved another chance after having lost to Mr. Roosevelt in 1944. The possibility of victory was promising. Former Vice President Harry Truman, who had succeeded to the office following Roosevelt's death in April of 1945, was thought to be "beatable" even though Truman had the advantage of being the incumbent. The Democrats were worried about the ability of this unsophisticated man from Missouri to challenge the more sophisticated New York Governor Dewey, who appeared to be supported with all the financial resources needed to win.

My most prominent memory of that political fight was Truman's decision to go on a "whistle stop" train tour across the country to rally the Democrats' vote. The newspapers carried lots of pictures of Truman waving from the rear of the train as he chugged across America and focused his campaign on the Republican-controlled House of Representatives and Senate by calling it a "do-nothing" Congress. Almost all the political news was in the newspapers in this last presidential election before television brought the conventions and campaigns into nearly every American home four years later. The outcome of the November election shocked the overconfident Republicans. Assuming a Republican victory, a major newspaper ran an early edition on election night with the very wrong headline "Dewey Defeats Truman," a headline Truman happily displayed after having won four more years in the White House for himself and the Democrats.

In 1952, as another election approached, political conditions were very different. The new Twenty-Second Amendment to the Constitution imposed a limit on how long presidents could serve. President Truman was barred from seeking another term. The office was open to either party and made for a much more interesting contest, a fight I followed closely as I delivered newspapers six times a week. Each day I absorbed the headlines as I folded papers tightly so they could be flung on more than a hundred front porches.

The Democrats found a candidate who was very different than the folksy and feisty Harry Truman. They chose the more bookish, less outgoing, and considerably more urbane Governor Adlai Stevenson of Illinois. Meanwhile, the Republicans were even more determined to have a candidate who could break the Democrats' twenty-year hold on the White house. At the outset of the campaign, it seemed the Republicans were going for Senator Robert Taft of Ohio, a veteran of national politics who had earned the title of "Mr. Republican." However, as I learned from the daily newspapers, the Republican nomination process became an increasingly brutal contest that was only settled after intense political infighting.

In the 1950's, many states did not have primary elections.

State politics were centered in the legislatures where powerful politicians from each party would gather and decide who would be their party delegates to the national conventions. That was how political control was exercised. Senator Taft had courted the powerful leadership in each state and won support that seemed to give him a tight grip on the nomination. Then his strategy fell apart.

A new potential candidate entered the competition, signaling the Republican party's intense desire for a victory. With great effort, the party persuaded Dwight Eisenhower to get into the race. A five-star general, the commander of the D-Day invasion and the supreme commander of all allied forces in Europe, Eisenhower had unassailable appeal if he could just win the Republican nomination. At the convention there were battles involving the legality of the way delegates to the conventions were chosen in some states. Eventually the fight came down to a stalemate between Ike and Taft. On the second convention ballot the votes swung in favor of Eisenhower who became the new standard-bearer, and Senator Taft would never realize his dreams of winning the White House. In the national campaign, Adlai Stevenson was no match for the American hero of WWII. The Republicans had finally achieved their long-sought victory.

Four years later there was even greater television coverage of the 1956 presidential election. The increasing number of states holding primary elections created a more interesting competition that could be watched on television in the months leading up to the conventions. There was fascination with the numbers of delegates won in each primary as candidates in both parties collected support for the nomination. The primaries had all the excitement of a horse race and by the mid-1960's, a point had been reached where the nomination of presidential candidates was generally a foregone conclusion before the Republican and Democratic conventions were gaveled to order in the summer preceding the November voting.

This transformation brought about by the television age revealed the historical importance of the Truman victory in 1948 and the Eisenhower win in 1952. A watershed in American politics had been reached that severely loosened the tight control of the nominating process by party leaders in the states. The decades from 1960 onwards were times of increasing numbers of registered voters as the eighteen-year-old voting age, the power of civil rights and the activism of all sectors of the population took on a more defined role. And churning away in the midst of this social change were ever more powerful computers for number-crunching that permitted analysis not just of party preferences but also preferences within genders, age groups, income levels, educational levels, geographic locations, and even more detailed influences on voter choice.

### *A History of Limitations on Political Participation*

Just as I was aware of the '48 and '52 elections, nearly all Americans are aware of presidential elections. They may only get involved by voting on election day, but they have opinions about which candidate they prefer. They decide based on information about the people who have competed for the nomination of their party, men or women who believe they are qualified to serve in the nation's highest office. The constant campaigning before the national conventions can exhaust these aspirants as they seek to persuade the voters that they have the "right stuff." Eventually, constant polling reveals who are likely to have a chance as others drop out when realizing their hopes are beyond their reach.

Underlying the excitement of presidential elections is the reality that our system of government was designed to keep individual citizens from meaningful roles in determining the outcome of elections in the states and to national office. Our history shows a persistent mistrust of the electorate and the creation of measures to control the numbers of eligible voters. Examples include:

- The Constitution provided for selection of congressmen by "electors" (voters) judged to have the qualifications in the various states. In 1776 in New Jersey, the qualifications were fifty English pounds. Each state had its own rules.
- The Senate of the United States was chosen by vote of the state legislatures until the passage of the 17th amendment in 1913 which required a popular vote of all voters in an individual state.
- Exclusion of women from voting was standard until passage of the 19th amendment in 1920, which guaranteed female suffrage.
- The Constitution made no provision for the rights of enslaved people, although each slave was counted as 3/5 of a person for purposes of calculating total population of a state to determine the size of its congressional delegation. The abolition of slavery under the 13th amendment, guarantee of the rights of citizenship under the 14th amendment, and the 15th amendment guaranteeing the right to vote began a redress of those conditions.
- However, during the period of reconstruction in the American South after the Civil War, African-Americans were denied voting rights in states due to Jim Crow laws

creating obstacles that would prevail until the last third of the twentieth century; the most notable law being the passage of the 1965 Voting Rights Act.

These legal limitations show how the practices of the American government were manipulated from the early days of the Republic. Change was achieved only after dedicated citizens and exceptional statesmanship overcame obstacles that resulted in the passage of constitutional amendments or critical legislation.

### *The Conservative Nature of the Electoral College*

The single most dominant example of how control was exercised over the American citizens, both voters and non-voters, was the system designed for choosing a president. The Founding Fathers had considerable reluctance to rely on a simple majority of all the votes cast (the popular vote) in all the states combined as a means for electing a president. To ensure greater control over the process they created the Electoral College which means we do not vote directly for the president. Today, in each of the fifty states, the voters select "delegates" to the Electoral College, men and women who then usually cast their votes in support of the candidate who has won the majority of the votes in their individual state in the national election. There are 535 "electors" equaling the number of 435 congressmen and 100 senators. This means a state having five congressmen plus its two senators would send seven delegates in the Electoral College.

Why did the founding freeholders create such a system? As noted earlier, they believed a simple national majority vote of all voters without regard to the individual states might fail to produce a majority for one candidate if there were several candidates. The Electoral College serves to control possibility of such an outcome. The successful candidate must win a majority of the 535 electoral votes based on ballots of the delegates from individual states. A president can win a majority of the national popular vote and still lose the election if he/she does not have a majority of delegate votes cast in the Electoral College. This occurred in the 2000 election in which Mr. Gore had a majority of the popular vote, but Mr. Bush won a majority of the Electoral College votes. Therefore, it is important to "win" a majority of the popular vote in states with the largest delegations that will produce a majority in the Electoral College.

This electoral system has the quality of preserving stability for the parties in power and allows them to exercise influence over results by controlling the politics in the individual states. Historically, the Founding Fathers wanted calm as do today's politicians. Chaos disrupts business and disturbs the economy. The Founding Fathers preferred a calm political landscape and succeeded by creating a system that promoted stability.

### *Preference for Majority Rule*

This brings us to our system of voting which emphasizes majority rule. In congressional elections, the candidate with the most votes wins. In a close race this means that up to half of the votes could be wasted. It is a system unlike other countries which practice "proportional representation" in which candidates can be elected based on the percentage of the vote a party receives. For example, if there was a proportional representation system in an American state there would be no congressional districts. The congressmen elected in a state would be based the percentage of the vote won by each party. If, based on population, the state was entitled to five congressmen and the vote was split 60/40 between two parties, one party would receive three seats and the other would receive two.

America does not use such a system and is unlikely to ever have one. Each congressional district elects just one candidate and the votes for the loser are essentially "wasted." This practice also preserves stability as it avoids many political groups competing for representation that could result in outbursts of instability. People will vote for the party with a likely chance of winning rather than "waste" their vote.

### *The Foundation of Our Party Politics*

The constitution makes no mention of political parties and the system we have is derived from a model developed in England. Those eighteenth-century English and American parties were not created to represent the whole population in either country. They were organizations to be used by the politicians who held elective office and the electors qualified to vote. Those elected officials were generally the people of means and wealth who wanted limited government. They were less interested in the needs of the majority of the population who were largely excluded from the political process. Historically and in the present day, American parties have always been organized to achieve two goals: (1) to promote the preferences of the governing elites and (2) to win victories in state legislatures, congressional elections, and presidential elections.

Since the creation of the Congress, the competing groups have been organized into "caucuses," a term still used today by the

Republican and Democratic parties in their congressional meetings. The two original "caucus" parties were the "Federalists," who favored more concentration of power in the national government, and "Democratic-Republicans," a party founded by Thomas Jefferson, which favored preserving power for the individual states to ensure the national government did not become too powerful. Eventually, the Republicans split from the Democrats and emerged as the Whig party until the middle of the nineteenth century, when they were succeeded by the creation of the Republican party. The one dominant feature of the system was the persistence of just two major parties. Created inside the Congress away from public view, they would emerge during election years to encourage those entitled to vote to support their differing views.

### *Preserving the "Caucus" Model of Political Parties*

Our historic American parties did not change even as more and more citizens became eligible to vote. They remained "caucus" parties with a continuing focus on winning elections, controlling the work of government by being "in the majority" in the Congress, and winning the presidency. Even as the country changed while it discovered positive activities for the government to address, beginning with public education, the party system remained the same. The growth of the population eligible to vote resulted in demands for services for the people and protection against practices dangerous to life. An example of social change was the growth of labor unions with demands that sought improved working conditions.

## *The Illusion of "National" Parties*

America still accepts the illusion of two "national" parties when it convenes presidential nominating conventions. Those conventions create party platforms that attempt to suggest there is national unity in each major party. In reality, elections in each of the fifty states involve both the two major parties but may also include minor parties. This creates more than one hundred state parties having different interests and political agendas depending on the various regions of the country. It is clear that predominantly Republican states in the South have different interests than Republican-dominated states in the Northwest. The idea of America having truly national parties only appears for presidential elections and soon fades after election day. Men and women elected to the Senate or the House of Representatives are free to pursue their own personal agendas in service to constituents in their congressional districts or the states they represent in the Senate. After elections, the caucuses of Republican or Democratic members of Congress reconvene in the U.S. Capitol and influence of the voters in the governing of the nation becomes less prominent.

### *Modern Threats to Political Control*

Changing a party's control of a congressional district has become increasingly difficult. As the boundaries of congressional districts are redrawn each decade, the results often favor the incumbents. This creates "safe" seats where the majority party in a congressional district can have a certain level of comfort that its control is secure. Challengers from the opposing party are at a disadvantage. Since the redistricting process is done by state legislatures, it is important for the major parties, Democrat or Republican, to win control of state legislatures and governorships in order to have control over shaping individual districts, which is done every ten years after a national census. Fortunately, there are legal rules that must be considered in doing the redistricting process to ensure that citizens are fairly represented. However, even these rules cannot always overcome politicians' determined efforts to make their party's dominance permanent. And for the voter going to the polls on election day, there is the real prospect of their voices not being heard if the district has been constructed so that one party has a clear advantage in winning before the polls even open.

The purpose of all this attention to re-districting or changing the boundaries of congressional districts is to preserve the tight-knit caucuses in the U.S. Congress by ensuring control of a majority of the seats of the 435 representatives and 100 senators. American party leaders make few demands on citizens, encouraging them only to register a party preference. Such an absence of control by parties over their registered voters has in recent decades created substantial risk. Lack of control has led to the increase in the number of voters registering as "independents," which causes a weakening of party influence on voter choice.

As the number of registered independents grows, these voters have been less likely to support a major party whose ideas do not meet their needs. This is worrisome to the caucus party leadership in both major parties. Independent voters create uncertainty and winning elections becomes harder for the party leaders controlling the congressional caucuses. With so many independent-minded voters providing critical votes that determine the outcome of elections, caucus parties must spend more money to encourage the support of not only their party members but also of registered independent voters.

## *Suppressing the Vote*

In the twenty-first century, the response to this election uncertainty has encouraged tactics to "suppress" the vote of citizens who are likely to vote against the candidate favored by one party or the other. The most well-known way to achieve this is for a state legislature to pass rules that make it more difficult for some people to register to vote. There are instances of states requiring excessive documentation to register to vote. The strategy of "voter suppression" is generally favored by politicians who prefer limited government that is less interested in expensive public policies. It is a replay of the tension between the historic freeholder notion that the "wisest and best in the society" are best suited for control. It preserves the historic models of caucus parties versus the demands from growing numbers of more independent-minded voters.

## *Major Party Stability and the Folly of Third Parties*

When congressional caucuses of both Republican and Democratic parties stubbornly refuse to compromise on serious issues, the public becomes frustrated. Demand grows for change in the control imposed by the two parties. One of the more popular ideas is the formation of new parties that could force an end to deadlock politics. However, this option rarely works in local or state politics, and is impossible at the national level for presidential elections.

Some of the examples of the failure of third parties indicate this lack of success. After retiring from the presidency, Teddy Roosevelt broke with the Republicans and founded the Bull Moose party to run for the White House as a third-party candidate in 1912. He failed. Southerners opposed to changes in civil rights laws started the Dixiecrat party in 1948 and ran Strom Thurmond for president. The party failed. John Andersen sought to run as a third-party candidate in 1980. He failed. Ross Perot created a third party in 1992 and drew wide support, but ultimately failed. The two-party system overwhelmingly favors the two major parties.

The unrest across the political landscape in 2008 gave birth to a more conservative element in the Republican party labeled the Tea Party which did not run its own candidate but sought to influence the Republican Party. In the 2010 congressional elections, the Tea Party was successful in influencing the politics inside the Republican Party after electing enough congressmen to form its own mini-caucus within the party. It has had an impact in influencing the policy choices of the Republican caucus leadership by withholding support on key issues, most notably budgetary matters. This has proven to be a successful strategy for gaining political prominence by working within an existing political party structure.

The growth of a successful third-party movement at the level of congressional elections, as represented by the Tea Party, shows that the caucus party system remains the dominant vehicle for controlling our political life. It ensures political control will reside in the 435 seats of the House of Representatives by electing individuals in districts that have been shaped by state legislatures to protect incumbents. If a Tea Party candidate can defeat an incumbent, the Tea Party suddenly has real power. The Tea Party was wise in not creating a separate party. Instead, it sought a home within the Republican party where it can have the most influence.

## *Predicting Winners and Losers in a Caucus Party Political Landscape*

Harry Truman's victory in 1948 had a notable technical aspect that affected the way we look at electoral politics. The popular predictions indicated that Dewey was going to win. He did not! Why? The academic world took notice and started its own inquiry. What they discovered was that few registered independents meant the major influence on voting choice was party registration. It turned out that when people went into the voting booth, the biggest influence on their choice was the party they felt they belonged to. It was a significant discovery. It created a solid baseline for the beginning of all the polling that now floods the television networks. As computers became more efficient, polling became more precise at predicting the political choices of smaller and smaller groups of voters. Also, as people stopped choosing parties and increasingly registered as independents, this precise kind of polling has become vital to political campaigns. This is because seemingly less popular candidates could win victories even in heavily defended districts by mobilizing identifiable groups based on computer data to offset the advantage which the holder of the "safe" seat thought he or she enjoyed.

### *Considering the Future of Our Party Politics*

In democracy's crowded house, the historic model of caucus parties currently survives despite the sophistication of modern technology and a more informed electorate. However, eventually the role of technology and the twenty-four-hour news cycle may diminish the influence of our historic party model by creating a means for the emergence of additional groups that can influence political control in state parties and weaken the historic control of caucus parties. When that will happen remains to be seen, but in a bit more than half a century we have come a long way, beginning with the Voting Rights Act of 1965, which was stimulated by the rising activism of the African-American community and growing demands for an economic system that was fair to all Americans.

There is a strong likelihood that wealthy interests will resist any loss of influence by using their wealth to support the survival of the historic party system. After all, it is a system designed with multiple means of preserving control: single-member congressional districts, indirect election of the president through the Electoral college, and state control over the shape of districts to create safe places for those already in power.

If you are thinking about active participation in political life, remember the system was designed to promote stability and order with a controlling influence by the wealthy. The response to such conditions of political control is greater citizen awareness to express opposition to interests that only serve the well-being of the few. Harry and Ike were beneficiaries of the system the freeholders built. The emergence of the Tea Party has demonstrated that a political movement can have an effect on change but will not succeed if it attempts to create a national third party. The rigidity and imperviousness of two-party politics is part of the enduring legacy the freeholders created more than two centuries ago.

# *Croquet, Quoits and Monopoly:*
## Using the Tools of Politics


Growing up in the 1940's without television meant lots of time for games played with family or friends. Our games were stored in a special cupboard and used after school, on weekends, and during vacations. Many of those indoor games had come from the farm where Dad grew up. The checker board was worn on the edges from decades of use. The dominoes from the farm taught a complex game helpful in learning to do math in your head. You only scored when the total on all the end pieces snaking across the table added up to a number divisible by five. Parcheesi taught strategy as we competed to get all our pieces to the center of the board.

Our outdoor games from the farm included quoits and horseshoes, which we played in the driveway alongside the house, learning to pitch "ringers" on the hubs twenty-one feet apart. We set up the croquet set on our sloping backyard each summer until Dad decided to build a good croquet pitch. It was not full-size, but it was level with carefully tended grass, a place where we learned croquet was a game of skill, strategy and some ruthlessness. When all the aunts, uncles, and cousins came for the 4th of July picnics, croquet games were serious events played by Dad and his four very competitive sisters.

Outdoor neighborhood games were disorganized play with a lot of made-up rules. There was no Little League. Organized baseball was for teenagers playing American Legion ball. Our neighborhood baseball games were mostly six-a-side played in Green Brook Park. At West End School the most organized game was dodge ball until we got to fifth grade and began to play softball. Hardball was a high school sport.

Games were seasonal. Touch football in the fall, shooting basketball hoops in winter, and baseball in spring and summer. We did not pay much attention to national sports teams, except for baseball. At our house we rooted for the Philadelphia teams, the Athletics and the Phillies. The Millstone farm where Dad grew up got the Philadelphia papers, so they were his teams and they became the family's teams. Professional football had yet to make an impression on our lives and we were generally unaware of professional basketball.

In the informal neighborhood play and the board games at home we learned important lessons about winning and wanting to win. In unsupervised chaos we sought to improve at outdoor sports and think carefully about how to finish on top in board games. We realized early that winning consistently took practice and thoughtfulness. Sometimes we got a hit or scored a touchdown or won at dominoes, Parcheesi, or checkers, but we understood how difficult it was to be consistently good.

### *Playing a Political Game*

One game we played for years did not come from the farm. That game was Monopoly! Made popular in the years of the Great Depression, it was based on a 1902 version called "The Landlord's Game." It seemed to be all about business, economics, and the strategies of buying real estate, mortgaging properties, and building houses and hotels to provide rental income. But it was really much more than just the economics of real estate. It was a game that had politics woven throughout it. Players went to jail, won beauty contests, received regular income just for passing "Go," and knew that their future depended on the luck of the dice. It allowed for accumulation of wealth through careful (and lucky) moves with the intent of gaining enough financial power to bankrupt the other players. If we were unlucky, we wound up owning Mediterranean Avenue. The winners had hotels on Boardwalk and Park Place. It was a game that taught fundamental lessons about life: The wealthy control outcomes! The wealthy have influence and power! Winning depends on making shrewd choices! The Community Chest, Chance, and Get-out-of Jail Free cards do not pay the rent on Marvin Gardens! Winning at Monopoly involved gaining power and influence by managing money. It was the most competitive of all our childhood games. We just did not realize how much we were learning about politics.

### *Politics Defined*

A simple definition of politics is: "**Politics is the public practice of either changing or maintaining conditions in our lives.**" That is what the Monopoly player is trying to do and what people engaged in politics are doing. In an election, the person in an office wants to be re-elected. The person challenging the incumbent wants to take the office away. People who do not like a rule or a regulation want to change it. Others who like the rules seek to keep things from changing. This is what is happening on school boards, town councils, municipal boards, county government boards, state legislatures, and the U.S. Congress all the time. In each case, people are working to change or maintain conditions of life. That's politics!

### *Political Power Defined*

Defining politics requires an additional definition explaining political power. The definition must show how the balance between existing conditions and new realities can be changed or preserved. It should also indicate how we distinguish between who is powerful and who is powerless. A rather long sentence provides an answer: **Political power is the ability to bring about desired change in conflict with and at the expense of others in the community, state, or nation.**

The powerful get what they want at the expense of those who have less power. And what is clear from playing Monopoly or learning the history of the wealthy in America, is that those with wealth tend to have greater influence in making people change their minds. Therefore, one of the key indicators of political power is the availability of financial resources. The owner of the hotel on the Boardwalk and the wealthy business owner seeking a change in zoning laws have more powerful positions than the Monopoly player with mortgages on all his/her properties or the farmer who does not want his acreage re-zoned for commercial development.

### *Applying Political Power*

When a political dispute exists, the people with power use their position to bring about change in two ways:

- **Voluntary compliance:** People can be persuaded to agree to change through peaceful persuasion, such as messages on TV or through other forms of media. If the messages are skillfully done, an individual, a school district, town, municipality, city, county, or state may agree that the suggested change is a good idea.

- **Limiting probability of enforcement:** When it seems unlikely that people will voluntarily change, the second way of exerting control is to suggest legal, forceful means of action such as lawsuits, financial penalties, or negative public messaging. Consider a simple example. At an intersection with a stop sign there is the possibility of a police car waiting on a side street to catch a driver who runs the stop sign. Drivers know that the police frequent that intersection but do not know if the police are there on a specific day. Therefore, drivers obey the stop sign because there is "the limiting probability" of receiving a ticket if they do not stop. We obey laws because the consequences of failure to do so carries a penalty.

Using these two approaches – voluntary compliance or threats of enforcement – the powerful can have those opposed to change either give in willingly or be threatened with consequences if they resist. This second method sounds scary, but it is the way politics works. The application of political power is a combination of persuasion or the threat of more serious actions.

### *The Source of Political Motivation*

The people who are willing to use political power are the same people who once may have been excellent Monopoly players. They learned early that winning requires the calculation of risk, patience, and hard work to produce desired results. They are also people who are inspired by the places where they grew up, the family lives they lived, the lessons taught by parents, and the values/preferences they desire most highly. Their youthful experiences translated into acquisition of the skills necessary to be professionally competent, and display the ability to earn respect from peers in order to "go into politics." The intentions of these politically-oriented people are planned so that notice will be taken and suggestions made that they would be good choices to serve in government as councilmen, mayors, congressmen, or even senators.

We know lots of people who have little or no interest in politics, much less a desire to be a politician. These men and women are quite happy to work as doctors, lawyers, bankers, businessmen, teachers, religious leaders, craftsmen, or administrators in public agencies – people content with a good life, respect in the community, good health, and time to constantly explore new areas of knowledge. They are not politicians.

In contrast, people who crave access to power find that their professional achievements and community recognition are not enough. They want influence over how the rules are made. They may have all the pieces of a good life, but they want political influence and the recognition that comes from being powerful.

In speaking about their goals in life, political people may say they are doing things to serve the public good, to improve the communities in which they live, or to make better lives for more people. And that may be true, but behind those announced lofty goals there is often a person who seeks power and is willing to use political skills to achieve their goal of having influence. In the rough-and-tumble world of politics at all levels, there is the old saying, "Politics ain't bean-bag!" It is also not dominoes, Parcheesi, checkers, quoits, croquet, or Monopoly. It is an experience demanding toughness of character to acquire the power so important to politicians.

### *Political Practices*

Wishing or hoping to lead an influential life is not enough! Achieving power depends on skills and talents learned in various places. Generally, the things we value lead us to institutions or organizations where we learn the skills we need. Once one has embarked on a political career, other skills and talents are acquired to advance one's personal interests. These skills and tools are of four types:

- images and symbols
- rational threats
- material goods
- emotional persuasion

When a politician's career is examined, examples can be found illustrating how these skills and tools were applied in the pursuit of political goals.

## Images and Symbols:

Political symbols can be images, words, and phrases that succinctly convey political messages to gain support for ideas. This is a standard practice in which some might say they are sharing information and others would say the symbols are propaganda. Use of symbols is a skill that requires awareness of how the marketing of images and ideas can be done. It is a psychological effort to persuade people with pictures, images, and carefully chosen words that link those ideas to people's emotions to successfully "sell" political ideas. The phrase is often used of "wrapping oneself in the American flag." It denotes the use of American flags as a symbol when making political appearances.

Lots of symbols are linked to patriotism and the nation's military history. Images and symbols are widely used to encourage support for a candidate for election, support for a particular law, or getting action from a government. Election campaigns are ideal examples of how symbols are used to manipulate voter's attitudes for or against a candidate. For example, candidates arriving at events in motorcades or landing in a plane are ways of suggesting the power and influence a politician possesses. The development of digital media expands ways to manipulate images in positive and negative ways to influence opinions and outcomes. Politicians know how to use symbols and images to shape the personal story of their lives and make themselves more attractive to voters.

Recent changes in laws now permit unlimited amounts of money to be spent on elections or campaigns on public issues. This means the use of symbols, whether accurate or inaccurate, are multiplied into tens of thousands of messages that can have a significant impact on the outcome of elections or political issues. This reality also demands that individual citizens make decisions on a candidate or an issue by scrutinizing the material being used to persuade voter's or citizen's choices.

**Rational Application of Threats:**

The use of symbols or images with psychological impact are linked to another tool of politics: the rational or calculated use of threats of violence in political disputes. The tool of political violence does not actually require physical action. The mere threat of violence can often achieve the desired outcome. Political groups can make threats if their goals are frustrated. There can be the threat of labor strikes, "go slow" or "work-to-rule" actions on assembly lines. Threats of legal action are a form of "rational use" of violence employed by politicians or businesses to win victories. The key tactic is to provide threats that are detailed enough as to put "the affirmation of doubt" in the mind of the people, a company, or an administration that is being pressured to change a position on a candidate or issue. The need to actually use physical violence is a sign that the "rational calculation" of a threat of physical action has failed. When analyzing political action, take care to examine how far politicians or political groups are willing to push the boundaries to achieve goals that do not conform to standards of democratic practice.

**Use of Wealth and Material Goods:**

The use of wealth to manipulate outcomes is a well-understood tool of politics. Money talks! Laws now allow individuals and groups to use unlimited amounts of money in their pursuit of political goals, and they do so in the most robust way. The creation of political action committees or PAC's is a part of all major political campaigns. In states that once had relatively insignificant amounts of money to fund presidential campaigns, PAC's now spend tens of millions of dollars to persuade the voters to pick a "well-heeled" candidate. It is true that "money is the mother's milk of politics," and presidential elections can now require the expenditure of over a billion dollars in total.

Money and anything else of value can also be used in various ways to influence outcomes. Bribes can be paid. Financial favors can be done on behalf of politicians to influence votes. Promises of financial support can be withheld if a politician does not vote the way he or she has promised. The provision of goods and services without the direct payment of funds is also a routine part of political action. Flooring is done at no cost to a politician, a street is newly paved in front of a politician's home, or an easement is granted so a politician can develop a property for commercial use. The list can be nearly endless in a system where the "freeholder mentality" prevails and so much of the wealth in America is controlled by 1% of the population who can commit vast sums to achieve outcomes that could not be won in public debate or at the ballot box. This reality requires serious effort to discover why politicians vote as they do and who might have provided either money or items of financial value to influence the outcome of an election or a vote on a critical public issue.

**Rules and Practices for Persuasion:**

**Knowing the Rules:** Successful politicians know an essential tool for winning is knowledge of all the rules of governing and engaging in political activity. Perhaps the most widely known set of rules are those used to conduct a meeting, for which a solid working knowledge of *Robert's Rules of Order* is necessary. A quick internet search provides a succinct listing of all the procedures that are employed in the use of Robert's Rules. Understanding how a meeting can be run gives great power. Meetings can be slowed down by asking repeated "points of order, points of information, or points of personal privilege." These are all actions that take precedence over any other item of parliamentary procedure being used in the conduct of a debate. Speeding up meetings can be accomplished by "calling the question," which means asking that that there be an immediate vote and suspension of debate. Because that request is non-debatable, it must be acted upon before any further business can be considered. A person may lose the vote when "calling the question" and the debate can resume, but the pace of the meeting has been slowed, which is sometimes a strategic advantage.

The arrangement of the agenda can also control a meeting. Announcing that an agenda will be considered *ad seriatum*, or "in the order in which items are printed on the agenda," means that certain controversial items can be taken up at the end of the meeting, after consensus has been achieved on earlier items. Agreement on previous items helps influence participants to accept the final items under review. Finally, if a desired outcome does not seem to be emerging, there can be a "move to table," meaning a decision can be put off until a later date. Knowing and applying these rules is a skill that can influence outcomes.

Knowledge of rules of procedure is linked to the way that the details of the meeting are recorded. Recording the minutes from the meeting provides another form of power, so being asked to be the "secretary" is *not* a thankless task! The person who takes the minutes controls history, shaping the way issues on the agenda were debated and recorded. While seeming neutral, the words in the minutes can convey messages that on later review may shift memories of what had actually been decided. Neutral-sounding but carefully constructed meeting minutes are an art form. One should never reject the opportunity to be the secretary as that person will have more long-term impact on the actions of the group than any speech given during discussion.

The importance of knowing the rules in community meetings is repeated in more complex ways as the responsibilities and importance of organizations expand. City councils and county boards of supervisors all have debates where manipulating the rules can be done to gain advantage for either side of an issuer. At the state government level, there are still more complex ways to manipulate the rule-making process. And the U.S. Congress is perhaps the most intricate rule-making body of all, with more than two centuries of history to draw on in finding "precedents" to apply to current debates in order to win victories for one faction or another.

Finally, there are the courts where our legal system provides many interpretations of the rules in order to gain victory in disputes. Our whole legal system is founded on the use of "precedents" that can provide differing interpretations of the law; cases and judgments can be cited in order to win a decision that sustains or reverses an existing law. Heated arguments arise as the original intent of provisions in the Constitution make their way through various levels of appeal to the U.S. Supreme Court for redress of grievance or affirmation of a desired condition. The use of precedents is often used in popular TV court dramas like *Law and Order*. While thousands of cases are filed with the Supreme Court each year, less than one hundred are likely to be heard. Nonetheless, arguing a case before the Supreme Court remains the most significant way in which knowledge of the rules can have an impact on political outcomes.

**Emotional Persuasion:** It may not seem like a political tool, but demonstrations can be effective when shrewdly used and can have an influence on political outcomes. A clever politician may actually welcome a demonstration in opposition to an issue the politician favors. A public protest can actually build support among fellow politicians to result in a favorable decision for the clever politician. For example, in 1973, Nixon sought to pass "The Safe Streets Act." Congressional support was in doubt. As Nixon left a meeting in California, protestors were present. Before climbing into his limousine, Nixon waved his hands in a victory symbol. The demonstrators responded by pelting Nixon's limousine with stones. The next day papers across the nation carried the headline: "President's Car Stoned!" As a result, public opinion swung in favor of the need for the Safe Streets Act. It passed due in part to Nixon's calculated use of emotions.

Demonstrations are also a means for large groups of people to "let off steam" and demand change. Politicians can gauge how long a protest is likely to last and may assume that the protesters will get tired, in which case they can be ignored. Only when demonstrators persist, start to elect leaders, and formally organize is it important to react seriously to such events. Otherwise, protests have a great "cathartic" effect and can be largely ignored while politicians make statements about having heard the protesters' concerns and promise to consider them. This is not an effort to discount the value of demonstrations. Nonetheless, it is important to realize that unless carefully done, demonstrations may have limited impact.

**Offering Condolence:** This is the last basic tool in a politician's bag of strategies. It is the attentiveness to emotional moments in political life. If there is a natural disaster, like a tornado, a hurricane, or a flood, politicians show up! If there is a man-made disaster, like a fire, the collapse of a bridge, or a horrific train collision, politicians show up! When a prominent person dies, politicians show up! When a tragedy affecting the lives of children happens, politicians show up! Politicians go to funerals, wakes, and memorials! Politicians practice being appropriately emotional! And politicians make sure to be seen being emotional! The message is that the important political person has made time in his or her schedule to be present and express sorrow at tragedy and comfort for the grieving. It is a rule that politicians master and use routinely.

### *Childhood Games and Political Games*

The games played by children have rules, even if they are sometimes made up, and there is a built-in fairness that comes from following those rules. In sports and board games, the rules are clear and any attempt to cheat can be discovered. Baseball is well-defined within the baselines. In tennis, being inside the lines is paramount. We learn to be competitive, but usually stay within the rules. Only when we are older do we learn how rules can be bent, such as pitchers putting substances on baseballs, athletes using steroids to be stronger and faster, and betting on contests leading to "fixing" outcomes. Our games as children were for fun. We had yet to learn the seriousness of sports.

Ideally, the practice of politics is an exercise in seeking to make a difference in public matters on behalf of communities and people. It can be approached in a high-minded civic way and great satisfaction can be earned from serving the public. However, we should be always aware that in settings where the stakes are high, there is a likelihood of using all means possible to secure a preferred outcome. Knowing the lives and backgrounds of the men and women in public life offers clues as to what tools each may be willing to employ in the pursuit of political influence. We must be attentive to the symbols, practices of persuasion, use of financial resources, and manipulation of the rules and popular emotions that are applied in political contests. Democracy's entire house is filled with the activities of competing interests and powerful personalities. In order to understand politics, issues must be broken apart and examined to understand just how they are being pursued and whether they are in the public interest.

# *The Courier News*
## Analyzing Political Realities

The *Plainfield Courier News* provided most of the news in our home. Occasionally Dad would bring home *The Sun* or the *Herald Tribune* from New York. When we were young, we only read the comics. The news was for our parents. Then a new routine for reading newspapers was begun in the fall of 1949 when I started delivering the *Courier News*. For two years I assisted Jan Peterson before he gave me the whole route of more than hundred customers. Each weekday I hurried home from school, folded the papers and headed off on my fat-tired Schwinn to the homes farthest from our house. The streets closer to home were the walking portion of the route and done last. Finished by 5:30! On Saturdays I finished a bit earlier. Six days a week for more than six years!

Delivering newspapers required reliability. When it rained the papers had to go in the mailbox or inside the storm door and kept dry while walking or riding in spring rains, summer showers and winter snow storms. Prompt deliveries and dry papers, however, provided job offers for shoveling snow, raking leaves, and cutting lawns. Also, "the route" taught me how to talk to grown-ups when collecting thirty cents a week from each customer.

The greatest financial reward for delivering papers came at the end of my senior year in high school. Based on school work and service to customers the Courier News, a Gannett publication, provided a $3000 scholarship. I was obliged to write a letter to Mrs. Gannett of the Gannett Foundation each year to inform her of my academic progress. In her last response to my letters she wrote, "Once you win a scholarship, you are 'our boys' from that moment forward."

### *The Best Reward: Habits for a Lifetime*

The Gannett Foundation scholarship equaled the cost of four years tuition at the college to which I had been admitted. That, however, was not the most significant reward the Courier News provided. Delivering papers for six years developed a habit of reading the news every day. This meant there was constant awareness of a complex world. Classroom learning in the 40's and 50's did not teach us about the migration of African-Americans from southern to northern states and the racism throughout our country. We were not taught about the poverty in Appalachia. Brief glimpses of a changing nation were only occasionally revealed in the Warner-Pathe newsreels at the movie theaters before the cartoons and the westerns movies on Saturday mornings. But the Courier News created a habit that continues more than six decades later as each morning I walk to the end of my driveway and pick up the paper that has been tossed there by some other early morning newspaper person in a slow-moving car making its way through the neighborhood.

Delivering newspapers exposed me to the most important stories in those times. Among the most prominent were the communist threat, the Korean War, the Eisenhower-Stevenson contest in 1952, the Rosenberg spy trial, and Senator McCarthy's investigations of suspected Communists in the government. His investigations falsely ruined the reputations of people but finally led to the humiliation of the senator when hearings in Congress made it clear he had misrepresented his claims with shoddy facts.

Those stories were lessons revealing the rough-and-tumble of political battles, showed how politics could be nasty, involve lies, reveal deceit, and create skepticism about the trustworthiness of some politicians. They also showed politics at its best when leaders enacted good policies and secured positive changes in American life. Truman implemented the Marshall Plan to rebuild Europe, integrated the military services, saved Berlin from Russian control, challenged the steel industry not to strike during the Korean War, and conducted himself as a man of the people. Earl Warren led the Supreme Court to a unanimous decision supporting integration of public schools. And Eisenhower proved to be a better president than we realized as he preserved calm at home while fighting the Cold War overseas. Those events were not in our school books, but they were on the pages of the Courier News.

I remember all these facts because I got into the habit of reading a newspaper every day. If you do not have such a habit yet, start! Just decide to read a newspaper every day. Why? Because that is where stories are covered in greater depth than a twenty-second snippet of film on a TV show. Newspapers offer a greater likelihood of providing important details about events happening to communities or individuals and describe specific actions being taken. Watching television can help, but reading newspapers is much more useful in shaping your judgments about political events.

### *No More Paperboys!*

The world of political news reporting that taught me politics has changed dramatically. In the 1950's we relied on local newspapers, three major TV channels and morning news on radio. Now we have hundreds of TV channels and all kinds of multi-media applications for use in the home, on phones, and with computers. To see a young boy or girl peddling through a neighborhood on a bicycle tossing daily papers on front porches is now less likely than finding someone still using an eight-track tape player.

This growth in the number of news services imposes a burden on every American trying to understand our politics as political opinions are dressed up as facts. Many television channels sell scripted messages claiming to be factual and designed to influence opinion on issues. Newspapers rely less on the reporting by their own staff and depend on information from wire services. The internet offers a true jungle of unsupported opinions and ideas for influencing elections and complex public policy. Finally, from abroad, foreign governments hack into computers to influence policy in a process now referred to as the "weaponization" of the media.

This increased difficulty in discovering what may be true makes political choices more difficult. The condition also defines the importance of all ideas shared in the earlier essays. Confronted with contradictory news, "weaponized" news, so-called "fake" news, and dubious political opinions requires focus on the basic realities that do not change: order versus freedom, the predominance of wealth in politics, the importance of an educated citizenry, and how political choices will impact the few versus the many. We are forced to more fully know the backgrounds and motivations of people who are seeking to shape political outcomes. In the twenty-first century, the gusher of real or compromised news is our daily examination for making judgments on the condition of our country and choices of matters that earn our support.

## *Making Sense of Political Facts*

The cascade of political information into our lives requires a personal means for slotting facts into a framework clarifying the link between new facts and old information stored in memory. An orderly system helps keep track of personalities, family legacies, and manipulation of political tools.

The creation of a framework of categories in which information is stored and easily recalled is the first step. Categories can be geographical, community-based, or focused on issues such as health, education, the environment, economics, and personal freedoms. The organization of facts provides the raw material for applying skills stored in our "toolbox" of ideas, which are used to analyze the meaning of all this information. Current facts are fitted together with historical knowledge as we examine each issue, election, and defense of our freedoms and values. What is clear as you start your study of politics is the importance of having a well-organized memory for old facts and paying constant attention to news and media to create an informed approach to understanding politics today.

One of the easiest models to use in studying political activity was created by David Easton, one of the most notable political scientists of the twentieth century. The usefulness of Easton's uncomplicated framework is relying on just six activities to examine the political environment. It can be used to understand a local referendum, a change in municipal real estate tax rates, disagreements over beautification projects, or legislative battles in Congress. The factors are divided into two groups of three each – "inputs" and "outputs." When using these inputs and outputs, think of them as a framework for the format of the daily quiz on political life, a quiz that asks who is engaged in political action, what are the values they pursue, and what are the tools they use to gain success in reaching their goals.

### The "Inputs" of Political Action

**The Message:** The first of the political inputs focuses on the intent of an idea. Words are important. Clarity counts. To influence results, messages must state what is desired and offer images of the consequences that might result if demands are not met. Correspondingly, political messages can also be deceptive, promising outcomes or misstating facts to cause embarrassment to opponents. The key question to ask is, "Will this message sell?" Is the message believable enough to gain widespread public support?

Political messages work best if they are brief and leave little doubt as to what is desired. The campaign slogan used by Bill Clinton in 1992 is a near perfect example: "It's the economy, stupid!" That was all that people needed to hear and it shaped a presidential victory. Phrases such as "Black Lives Matter!" encourage sympathy but do not suggest how to achieve victories. Candidate Barack Obama used the simple phrase, "Yes, we can!" to imply hope, the capacity to achieve goals, and group effort by referencing "we." Message-makers are intent on influencing outcomes. They are not playing Monopoly or bean bag! So, listen to the messages as they contrast with other news sources and decide if they are real or fake!

**Political Support:** The second input is support for the message. The analysis shifts to how support is gathered among larger and larger groups of people willing to share the message and approve of action being taken to support the message. Basically, it is answering the question of who is in favor of the message! This is where opinion polls reveal how a message is being received. Polling has become an art form permitting political messages to be fine-tuned to influence small segments of a population. During presidential campaigns, polling has reached a state where polls can be generated daily to develop additional support.

There are various kinds of groups that can provide support. While uncoordinated demonstrations can have some value, the more valuable groups are organizations that can be recruited for special topics, such as health or education issues. Community associations or parent-teacher associations would fall into this kind of group. Testing the influence of a message requires examining the support it is receiving from political parties, professional associations, unions, and any organization with permanent staff, offices, and the sources of income devoted to realizing its political goals. Lastly, there are the most powerful message-carriers of all. These are administrative groups like government agencies that are organized for long-term service and in command of resources to make the most effective cases in advancing a message.

Politicians know how to use groups effectively. They depend on permanent organizations like political parties, lobbyists, and unions or professional groups. They also know they must get to key administrative people who may be persuaded on a course of action. A good politician will rarely depend on just demonstrations or occasionally-interested citizens. This is true at all levels of government, and it explains how administrative institutions win victories. In America's federal government, the Department of Defense is a good example of a permanent institution that knows how to get winning results from the US Congress. But, they use a similar kind of influence as a local school administration that has set a course and plans to build only one middle school instead of two.

**Broadcasting the Message:** The third input focuses on techniques used in broadcasting messages. It focuses on the ways in which the idea is presented to larger and larger groups of people through media. The message must be shaped into clarity, resources need to pick up the message and spread its acceptance among groups of people, and reports of the message and its growing acceptance must be presented in newspapers, radio, television, and social media. This is the most rapidly growing field in politics as facts are "weaponized" for less than neutral use. The skills applied to editing information into both positive and negative messages and manipulating messages can influence the outcome of close elections, provide margins of victory in referendums, and compromise or destroy the careers of public servants and elected politicians.

Trying to distinguish fake "weaponized" messages from straight-forward reporting is a difficult task. The key is to ask the basic questions about freedom and order. Who is hurt? Is this for the few or the many? Who benefits? Those three questions should help you develop thoughtful opinions on political issues.

## *Political "Outputs"*

**Making Rules:** Rules are developed by town councils, county executive boards, state legislatures, and congressional lawmakers. Those groups process the demand, expressed interests, and possible needs expressed in the messages, group action, and media flowing from the "inputs." How the rules are made can be complex, as each rule-making body has its own framework for considering new ideas, debating and amending ideas, and voting on ideas. At each stage, there are places where politicians can seek to manipulate the details of a rule to serve their own interests.

It is also a place where outside interests can intrude in the form of witnesses offering expert testimony and administrative experts who use their skills to draft new rules in advantageous ways. Lobbyists and professional groups also seek to insert ideas into a legislative process to serve their narrow interests.

Following the process of legislation is time-consuming and what is reported is not always what has happened, as deals are made out of the public view. Newspaper reporting is more adept at discovering what is really happening because they can more fully develop topics. Again, the guideline for examining the development of rules is asking the basic questions of who benefits and has the public interest been served?

**Applying Rules:** Once a rule or new piece of legislation has been approved, it passes to the bodies responsible for administering that new set of ideas. The process of implementing new mandates by local government, county administrators, state agencies, federal bureaus, or departments also provides opportunities for politics to intrude into the application of a new law. The rule-makers may have described the new law without sufficient detail and administrators have discretion on interpretation of a law. They can set down the terms of application, which may make it more difficult for the new law to serve its intended purpose. Politicians will seek to influence this application process by questioning the language of the new law or statute. Administrators are obliged to faithfully administer the laws as written, but any lack of clarity provides opportunities for political distortion. Again, the interpretation of the law as to whether it is serving its intended purpose is a point for inquiry and the making of a judgment on the fairness of the administrative process.

**Judging Rules:** Once new rules or laws have been put into place, disputes can occur as to the consistency of new law with past rules and regulations. This can lead to lawsuits being presented to the courts for examination. The courts have discretion in considering these cases and can either affirm the new law or dismiss it as a violation of a community's rights, state's rights, or constitutional rights. No matter how the courts rule, it is likely that some group will be unhappy and seek to change the condition by proposing new rules. For example, the history of legislation and court rulings on right-to-life cases is a measure of how lengthy the process of legal review can be.

Making rules is a very difficult job for Congress because laws apply to the entire country. Federal laws can impact healthcare, the official minimum wage, housing regulations, environmental practices, workplace safety, and dozens of other conditions in our daily lives. Arguments about the fairness of these laws can be contested in terms of how they are applied by administrators or made the basis of lawsuits that are brought to the courts. Court decisions can sustain the law or overrule it, and thus require that it be changed. When a law or a rule is changed, those who thought it was a good rule are disappointed. When a law is sustained, those who believed it was unfair are disappointed. Litigation on pro-life versus pro-choice issues over the years is a prime example of this process in politics.

Then the political activity starts all over again. For those who feel they have "lost" because a rule was changed or not changed, the six activities of political life begin again. The "losers" present a better idea, build greater support for a new rule, and work harder to broadcast and publicize the need for a change in rules. The idea is written in a new format, discussed by the rule-makers, possibly winning support, and then applied if approved. This can result in a whole new group of people who feel they are the "losers," and the political process continues. Politics is a never-ending cycle of people seeking to have the communities, states, and nation operate the way one group or another believes is best. It is always a balance between freedom and order. It is also a portrait of how freedom and order are in constant conflict. And if you read a newspaper each day and hold to the rule of asking who benefits and if the public interest is well-served, a thoughtful opinion will emerge.

### *Considering the News*

As we absorb the news and engage in our daily exams on how well we understand what is occurring, it is apparent that all the political tools can be routinely applied in various ways. The politicians, the practitioners of politics who come from interesting backgrounds, are observed as they are driven by the need to acquire power and influence and can be seen manipulating the "inputs" and the "outputs" of politics at all levels. Having a framework at hand for examining the six elements of the political system, as well as the symbols, threats, payoffs, rule manipulations, public emotions and use of condolences at events of tragedy and sorrow offer a way to know just what is going on. A daily newspaper and all other sources of information chronicle how the human condition is managed in America's political life. When you think about a political issue try to calculate all the tools for persuasion that are being applied. They can be found and read about each day in the Courier News six decades after I delivered my last newspaper.

# Part Five:

# Political Responsibilities

## *Offering Envelopes*
### State of the Union and Soul of the Nation

I can easily recall memorable church services. Each year as small children, we anticipated Christmas with poinsettias and evergreens in the cold of December, Easter with palm fronds and lilies, and Children's Sunday in June. Even the youngest children attended all these services in the sanctuary. The services had different messages, but the ceremony of offerings was always the same as shiny plates were passed through the pews, envelopes were gathered, and we all stood to sing the Doxology.

When I was seven, Mrs. Oghrin, my Sunday school teacher, explained I would be given a box of envelopes into which I would put my weekly offering. The offering was my contribution to the work of the church. From a weekly allowance of fifty cents, I put a dime into my collection envelope each Sunday. Mom usually gave me my allowance on Saturday, so there was always money for the offering. Those offering envelopes were my introduction to stewardship as a part of my religious faith. This responsibility was added to the activities of church life, including Sunday school, children's choir and senior choir to strengthen my belief in the Church's teachings such as being blessed by grace, praying for the well-being of all people and the world, and having a renewal of spirit in the act of communion. As a child, I did not fully realize how these acts of faith were shaping my life, including my obligation to active stewardship.

The habits of church life grow over time from nursery classes to Sunday choir, youth groups, and eventually membership in the congregation. If that faith commitment remains strong, individual faith life will be robust. However, when realities of life intervene, our church commitments may diminish. This is especially true of a weakening sense of stewardship. In providing collection envelopes to a seven-year-old, the Grant Avenue Presbyterian Church sought to create a willingness in me to support the congregation throughout my lifetime. In the church vestibule I found the box of envelopes with my name printed on it indicating, "this is part of your responsibility to the church and your faith."

The message was clear. Churches and congregations survive not just on prayer and expressions of commitment by the faithful. Churches, synagogues, mosques, and any other faith communities need financial support. Some congregations expect members to "tithe" a portion of their wealth. Each year, appeals are made to members of a congregation to pledge resources to meet many needs. Without those commitments, congregations may wither and dissolve. Prayer, reading scripture, regular attendance, and participation in church life are important. But committing to contribute money from one's pocket is vital. My weekly gift of a dime when I was seven was twenty percent of my allowance. When I had a paper route that provided six dollars a week, my envelopes contained at least a dollar.

### Democracy, Our Secular Faith

Growing up in America during the Second World War taught us children other forms of stewardship, which were similar to the weekly offerings at church. In elementary school, my classmates and I gave to the Red Cross, the Community Chest, and the March of Dimes. The Community Chest had a "Red Feather" logo, and our donations earned each of us a small plastic red feather to wear. For the March of Dimes, we had little cardboard "wallets" to fill and the principal would announce at an assembly how much money had been raised for the effort to cure polio. That effort became very real for the whole school when Billy Freeman, who was in my class, got polio. Billy's mom was my den mother for Cub Scouts. We had our meetings at his house because Billy could not move around easily. Billy died when we were in eighth grade.

Other activities in school were similar to the lessons taught in Sunday school because they were designed to build our faith in democracy. It was training in "citizenship." Saying the Pledge of Allegiance each day celebrated our country's values. Singing "God Bless America" reminded us of how lucky we were to live in this country. Lincoln and Washington's birthdays celebrated our American heroes. Veterans' Day and Memorial Day honored all who had served in wars. From first grade on we had social studies to teach us how America worked. Our social studies classes were like a confirmation class preparing us for participation in political life when we reached adulthood.

It is easy to see the parallel between lessons for our religious faith and lessons to strengthen our faith in democracy. Our American democracy is a secular religion, celebrating the virtues of freedom and equality. It is a faith made strong as we express support for our government and the laws that protect the rights of citizens, value the guarantees of equality before the law, and celebrate the freedoms that reside in the Constitution.

The Declaration of Independence and the Constitution serve

as a "catechism" for teaching the blessings of liberty and the obligations of citizenship. Like the intensity of our religious faith, the strength of our belief in America's democracy is a measure of how deeply lessons from our childhood remain in our adult lives. We also know that when our secular faith is abandoned or rarely practiced, our democracy is weakened as people fail to remain informed about political life or participate in the duties of citizenship. When millions of eligible voters do not show up at election time, democracy is diminished. When the turnout for primary elections is low, democracy is impaired.

### Threats to Our Democratic Faith

Human nature is complex. Individuals who are unconcerned about the fundamentals of democracy can still be fascinated with how our democratic freedom can be manipulated to achieve personal goals. Family backgrounds and youthful experiences can be influential in shaping personal agendas utilizing their education and professional skills to acquire influence. Such people who single-mindedly seek power are likely to be poor stewards of our democratic faith as they use money, legal (and possibly illegal) schemes, clever or patriotic symbols and actual threats to secure the goals they crave. And, in an era where new judicial decisions have removed any limit on the amount of money that can be spent on politics, these people may profess concern for the poor while seeking personal power and wealth.

Like people wandering away from their religion, Americans can lose touch with their democratic faith and embrace beliefs focused on pursuit of other values, the most prominent of which is wealth. When the "catechism" of democracy is vibrant and well-taught, our faith is maintained. When social studies or civics becomes less important, the foundation of our democratic faith is weakened. Too often, young people leave school with a limited understanding of how the country operates. Instead, they have far too many persuasive images of how wealth can be pursued for personal gains. When that happens, willingness to tithe or pledge to contribute to the needs of our democracy dissipates.

The parallel between sacred and secular religions is clear. Religious faith requires followers to make contributions to collection plates each week. They believe those donations will serve good purposes even if they do not know how much will be spent locally and what will be directed to good works for those most in need who may not even be members of the congregation. In the same fashion, faith in our democracy requires regular financial support. Americans may balk at such commitments, seeing payments to government as an obligation they would prefer to avoid. The lesson here is simple: Our faiths require tithes and pledges of wealth to remain vibrant and active. All who reside in democracy's house must affirm their secular faith by providing financial resources so that America's unique heritage will continue to be vibrant and active in each succeeding generation.

### *Celebrating Our Democratic Faith*

All religious traditions affirm their commitments to Protestant, Catholic, Jewish, Muslim or other faith communities. Each faith has important days of celebration and renewal of the spirit. Religious rituals preserve the strength of individual faith through confession and the solace of private meditation. Our democratic faith also has traditions for celebrating the nation's history and its achievements. Homage is paid to those who have given their lives in service to the nation. Each interment of a fallen warrior is done with a solemnity acknowledging sacrifice. More cheerful celebrations occur when people are granted citizenship, swearing their allegiance to the nation and the principles woven into the fabric of American life. Joy abounds as new citizens enter into full residency in democracy's house.

More recently in America, a time has been consecrated for the singular purpose of quiet renewal of faith in our democratic system. It is a special day for confessing a failure to fully realize the values of our democracy in our own lives and to rededicate the spirit to the principles of our democratic faith. That day set aside for reflection, remembrance, reaffirmation and dedication was formalized in an act of the U.S. Congress designating the third Monday in January for the celebration of Martin Luther King Jr.'s birthday. Following Dr. King's assassination in 1968, there was public enthusiasm to recognize Dr. King's contributions to American life. The action of Congress in 1983 established Dr. King's birthday as a federal holiday. Some states were initially reluctant to accept this congressional mandate, but by 2000 every state in the union was committed to setting aside the January date for the recognition and celebration of the life and legacy of Martin Luther King.

What is the real meaning of this day? In many respects, it is our annual referendum on the State of the Nation's Soul. It is a time when we recall the efforts of King, the Drum Major for Justice, who captured the spirit of the nation's soul in the 1963 "I Have a Dream" speech. If you have not considered it before, pause for a moment to think about what Martin Luther King Day really is. It is a solemn but celebratory referendum for measuring where we are in realizing the ideals of America.

Across the land, sermons and speeches promote equal rights for all Americans, regardless of differences. Prayer breakfasts begin early in what W. E. B. DuBois once called the "dusk of dawn." Schools spend the day teaching about the work of Martin Luther King, Jr. and the struggle against racial segregation. Other Americans spend the day volunteering in service to the community. In Arizona and New Hampshire, the day is combined with Civil Rights Day and in Idaho with Human Rights Day. This is a day of prayer to remind us of the need for national reconciliation among all people and inspired by a man who wore no uniform, won no military battles, and held no elective office.

### *Reporting on the State of the Union*

The referendum on our nation's soul achieves greater significance by the fact that it occurs close to one of the president's constitutional duties: the State of the Union Address. Article II, Section 3 of the Constitution requires the President "shall from time to time give to Congress Information of the State of the Union." In 1933, the Twentieth Amendment to the Constitution changed the date for the opening of Congressional sessions from March to January and moved the presidential inauguration day from March 20th to January 20th. President Roosevelt began a tradition of delivering the State of the Union Address during January, which has resulted in the State of the Union Address occurring close to Martin Luther King Day.

The President's State of the Union speech is a message to Congress to "recommend to their Consideration such Measures as he shall judge necessary and expedient." Those speeches reveal concerns for the needs of the people, reports on the economy, comments on foreign policy issues, and tend to outline budgetary priorities. In many respects, these addresses are reports on the fiscal and economic well-being of America.

Consider the accidental legislative linkage of these two key dates on America's annual calendar. The words and thoughts reaffirming the strength and power of our secular democracy are presented in a report on the state of the union. Correspondingly, within the space of a few days of the State of the Union Address all Americans engage in a day to vote with their voices, songs, prayers, and acts of generosity of spirit on the state of the nation's soul. The link between American ideals and the obligation to invest resources in our nation are bound together in the first month of each new year.

The annual referendum on the state of the nation's soul ought to be the springboard for the governmental agencies to be renewed in their efforts to make judgments and provide resources on behalf of the national interest and the well-being of all people in democracy's house. If such a linkage of messages on the national soul and the state of the union are congruent, we would approach each new year with a sense of purpose that is focused on doing the nation's business on behalf of all Americans.

### *Citizenship in Defense of Democracy*

Dedicated citizenship is not an easy task. As the Founding Fathers well knew, we are all imperfect people and subject to the temptations that accompany authority or responsibility. Counselors of law must be vigilant. Judges must be attentive to ensuring fairness and equity for all citizens and cast aside the claims of those who would seek to twist ideas and laws to personal gain or influence. Those entrusted with the tasks of making rules must pause in their deliberations and constantly ask if their actions are good for the "soul of the Union" and the "state of the Union."

If the twin obligations of "soul" and "fiscal well-being" guide the investments of time, energy, intellect, and wealth for maintaining and preserving the strength of our communities and country, then resources will be available to ensure our poor are fed, our weak and infirm are cared for, our young educated, and the security of our land never doubted. When surpluses are realized, they must be stored up for times when conflagrations destroy communities, tornadoes rip across America, hurricanes threaten or winter storms leave too many isolated in desperate need. Surpluses are the bulwark against shortages in municipal services, inadequacies in learning environments, and deficiencies in healthcare. For both the soul and character of the Union, citizenship involves a willingness to contribute an abundant granary of resources so there is enough to suffice during years when extreme need descends on the land.

## The Current State of the Union and Its Soul

It is apparent in too many ways the nation's soul is suffering. When children go to bed hungry our soul is compromised. When health care is not provided to all, especially the weak, the elderly, and the infirm, our soul is weakened. When we care not how equality and justice are dispensed to all the people in democracy's house, America's soul shrivels. When the wealth of the nation does not redeem all the promises for all the people, the nation's soul withers. Today the soul of America is not as wholly vibrant as our future requires. And if the soul of the nation is found wanting, then the state of the union is also found wanting. No celebration of stock market rises, no accounting for the great wealth of a small number of elites, no claim that all is well for democracy's house is legitimate or accurate as long as our soul does not reflect such realities.

The State of the Union speech and the national referendum each Martin Luther King Day are linked in time. Neither can be truly celebratory unless both reflect our ideals and promises made to all people. Preaching and prayers are not enough to sustain our national faith. There must be willing fulfillment of pledges of individual wealth to support the nation. If that does not happen, we will not have the country we want for our own lives and the future generations who will take up residence here. Fulfilling our financial obligations, offerings placed in symbolic collection plates, is essential for the future of democracy's house.

## *The Rent Is Due*
### Meeting Democracy's Costs

On the street where I grew up every family owned their homes
or had a mortgage. When the war ended, the few remaining vacant
lots soon became home-sites and more neighbors moved onto the
street. It was rare for a family to move away. I just assumed this
permanence was the way of life and only became aware some
people rented their living spaces when delivering papers in three-
story buildings and walking to a second or third floor to do the
weekly collections.

My family bought our house in a year that was considered the
second steep economic decline of the Great Depression. A notice
appeared in the *Plainfield Courier News* that read:

> 428 CATALPA AVE., corner plot 100 x150. Well-
> planted and amply shaded, older type home but in
> excellent neighborhood. We believe $350 down
> and $22.95 monthly will enable you to own this
> property which has unlimited future possibilities.

Some money my mom received from her father's estate
provided the down payment and a mortgage from the Plainfield
Savings & Loan Bank. Another small note appeared in the *Courier
News* in November of 1938:

"SOLD to John W. French and his wife, property
at Catalpa Avenue and Chestnut Avenue,
North Plainfield."

My parents lived in that house until 1983, when they moved into a nursing home. It was my home until I graduated from college. The mortgage was never paid off during those forty-five years as refinancing paid for renovations. Part of the front porch was enclosed to create an extra bedroom, radiators in every room replaced in inefficient coal furnace, new hardwood floors were added, and an extension on the back of the house expanded and remodeled the kitchen and added a screened porch that became an outdoor living room in the summer.

All around our neighborhood, houses seemed to go up everywhere. Many new homes were built along Willow Avenue, West End Avenue, and Rock View Avenue. My paper route expanded as almost every house took the *Courier News*. A handful of larger, older apartment buildings provided apartments in which renters leased their living spaces.

### In Search of a Reasonable Solution

Every American understands the idea of rent! If you lease a space you know what monthly rent payment is. To develop a solution to democracy's financial challenges, including accumulated deficits, a solution is needed that can be understood by all citizens. That solution must be (1) simple in design, (2) effective in performance, and (3) easily understood so that every citizen can say, "Yes, I 'get' that! It's an idea that can solve America's economic problems!" My solution is reasonable in design, clear in its intent, and not burdensome to individual residents. It is the demand for the collection of **rent.**

### Democracy's Leasehold

Living in America is like leasing a home. At birth, we become democracy's leaseholders, beneficiaries of the opportunities that life in America provides. But we are not the owners. We are temporary residents. For this exceptional privilege, it is reasonable for each of us to contribute to maintaining the quality of democracy's house. Freedoms, equality, and guaranteed rights exist only if honored and defended. Those conditions are preserved if we take care of democracy's house so it can be passed on in good condition to new generations of leaseholders - our children and our children's children. We are bound by the lease conferred upon us at birth or when granted the legal privilege of living in this land as immigrants or others. Currently, these lease agreements are held by over three hundred million people in democracy's house with its crowded front porch and in all the many rooms within its rambling structure.

### The Terms of the Lease

Democracy's leasehold contains a guarantee of the unalienable rights and political ideals embedded in our Declaration of Independence. However, our lease agreements are similar to our unalienable rights that offer terms and conditions that are implied or explicitly stated in both the Declaration of Independence and the Constitution. The implied obligations of democracy's lease include a responsibility for each of us to contribute to the maintenance of the property by making reasonable and productive political choices, such as voting thoughtfully, speaking up on issues of concern and obeying the law. Incorporated into our Declaration of Independence and the Constitution is the expectation of living meaningful lives. The Bill of Rights defines freedoms as well as constraints on residents. As one of democracy's "lease-holders," each person carries a responsibility to invest his or her financial resources to support and sustain those unalienable rights for the enjoyment of all who reside here.

## *The Founding Fathers' Creation of Democracy's Lease*

The idea that our democracy places lease obligations on each of us may seem like a radical notion in the same way that the Declaration of Independence was once a radical set of ideas. Lease obligations embedded in our founding document may not have been apparent in 1776, but they are there and they provide a basis for fulfilling promises made almost two-and-a-half centuries ago. Americans know our founding documents provided breathtaking freedom when compared to the harsh authoritarianism in eighteenth century Europe. Of course, among the original purposes of our founding documents was the intent to grant freedom to support the aspirations of men focused on small governmen, with just enough restraint to ensure their businesses and commerce could flourish. It was a model of government suited to late-eighteenth century conditions.

However, those documents also contained the elements of democracy's lease obligations incorporated into the promises of "life, liberty, and the pursuit of happiness." Those guarantees ultimately created an expensive model of governing if its principles were to be upheld for all citizens. What seemed like an inexpensive choice in 1776 gave way to expanded obligations of government in the nineteenth century as progressive liberal thought led to the public's conclusion that government ought to provide for more services beginning with public education. From that point on, the cost of governing has grown exponentially and continues to grow today.

The guarantees of personal liberty contained in the first ten amendments to the Constitution – the Bill of Rights – sought to satisfy the doubts of Americans who feared their individual freedoms might be eroded. Those amendments promised protection as people gathered, worshiped, and spoke against unwarranted use of authority while being secure in the knowledge of freedom from unreasonable search and seizure, right to protection in the courts, security of their homes, and the right to retain arms in their households. Those guarantees meant every citizen also had to respect the rights of every other citizen and given the right to have arms accept an obligation to defend the nation in time of peril. Taken together, those amendments contain not only guarantees but obligations that clearly inform each leaseholder of the terms of the lease.

### Democracy's Unalienable Lease Terms

The terms of democracy's lease are not debatable. Unalienable rights cannot be portioned out or divided to suit the wishes of an individual. Each person's responsibility for his or her lease agreement is for the total package that life in democracy's house provides. This reality is the foundation for determining individual lease costs for each American. It also means that rents will be variable depending on the degree to which America has contributed to the prosperity of each individual, since wealth was used to determine citizenship eligibility as a "qualified elector" (voter) participating in the politics of the 1700's. Success in each person's life is a matter of initiative, determination, creativity, hard work, and wise use of resources. If a person becomes wealthy, he or she should be entitled to keep a large portion of his or her wealth. However, the individual, whether rich or only modestly successful, must still be responsible for paying "the rent" on his or her lease for living in America.

### *Paying Rent Versus Paying Taxes*

Proposing that each citizen ought to pay rent is a big step. People have become comfortable with living "rent-free" in democracy's house for more than two centuries. Americans already pay taxes and generally believe they pay too much. However, it is also apparent that America does not collect sufficient revenue to meet the expenses of such a large country. We are told America is trillions of dollars in debt. To avoid wrangling over the provisions in America's large and complex tax code, it is much simpler to establish a second stream of revenue based on sound constitutional principles. The legitimacy for such principles is embedded in our founding documents providing for the creation of formal lease agreements requiring rent be paid as a cost of enjoying democracy's promises guaranteed to all citizens. In return, the rent paid will be used to keep democracy's house in excellent repair.

Let's be clear. Rent fulfills the lease agreement to maintain our democratic way of life. In contrast, taxes support state and local governments, which carry out the routine tasks of governing and providing agreed upon services. **Taxes** can be seen as the utility costs that any tenant pays, which are separate from the **Rent**, that guarantees residence for life.

American political life involves the constant argument that

taxes ought to be lower. Few remember that in the Eisenhower administration the country had tax rates as high as 90% on personal incomes. Intense political pressure constantly seeks to reduce these "utility costs" by granting deductions, special considerations, or other "loopholes" in the tax code. Over time, lowering taxes reduces revenue and increases deficits. Those deficits then cause expenditure cuts to create required "balanced budgets" at the state level, increased borrowing by the United States government, and a national debt of trillions of dollars. A tax solution to America's problems will not work because rewriting the tax code is too political a task and code provisions are generally not directed toward producing adequate revenue. Nearly three decades have passed since America overhauled its tax code. The political complexity of tax reform suggests an alternative means of revenue should be considered. That revenue stream needs to be based on constitutionally sound principles of lease obligations for enjoying unalienable rights.

### *Calculating Democracy's Rent*

People who live in leased housing know precisely when the monthly rent is due. Each person who leases space makes agreed-upon rent payments. This raises the question of how democracy's rent or lease costs for each person should be calculated. Again, the Founding Fathers provided an answer.

The Founding Fathers established the principle of calculating lease costs by using wealth as the variable for determining participation in the process of governing. In colonial New Jersey, the costs were set at fifty English pounds for a person to be considered eligible to vote and a thousand English pounds to run for election to a political office. From our nation's founding, wealth has been the measure formally permitting or less formally assessing the suitability of a person's participation in democracy's form of government. Based on that history, it is entirely reasonable to consider residency in America's house as subject to monetary obligation.

The idea of paying rent in order to determine how the freedoms of American life can be enjoyed is as old as the nation, and the method for calculating today's rent can therefore be "indexed" based wealth. In other words, the greater a person's financial success the greater the size of the rent payment. And this rent should be separate from the taxes paid annually. This rent would ensure democracy's house is always in good repair and capable of being expanded to accommodate future generations.

Democracy's lease costs would logically **exclude** loopholes, set-asides, deductions, and legislative magic to modify and reduce the rent assessed. The amount owed should be based on the rewards of being able to live in America and also be a testimony to the grateful stewardship each of us has for our democracy. Once the rent is paid, attention can be given to the more mundane and politically conflicted demands of paying taxes owed to governing bodies in communities, states, and the nation.

### *How Much Is the Rent?*

And how great might a rent payment in support of our democracy be? If the historic measure of fifty to a thousand pounds in colonial value is converted to today's monetary values, the rents would be commensurate with today's costs of living. For those who have prospered greatly, their rent should be greater. For those whose incomes are very small, their contribution would be small. Most importantly, the rent payment should be a testimony by each individual of his or her stewardship for all the blessings our democracy has conferred on their lives.

If America wanted to realize an additional two trillion dollars a year from its more than three hundred million residents, calculations indexed against income could soon produce a profile of how much ought to be paid at various income levels. Depending on income, the burden on any individual should be a modest inconvenience. At the upper ends of the income scale, it would represent no burden at all. Clearly, the rental costs should be differentiated on the basis of how living in America has provided rewards for the people who enjoy the privilege of living in here. The purpose is to derive several trillion dollars to which every resident contributes without necessarily compromising the ability of each person to also pay for the "utilities" of residency, their income taxes.

The actual amounts owed should be significant for those who have been blessed by the benefits of their leased residency in America's democracy. The greatest obligations would fall on the wealthy. There has always been a chasm between the success of average Americans and the success of elites who compile great fortunes by use of the laws they introduced. In recent decades, the width and depth of that chasm between wealthy elites and the majority of the leaseholders has grown measurably larger, reaching a point where individuals question why the promises of democracy are being withheld from the many in favor of the advantages to the few.

### The "Whitewashed" House

The wealthy in American society would prefer to shrink the role of government in people's lives. Many believe there should be less government oversight of environmental protection, safe food, and pharmaceutical products, or the intricacy of banking transactions and commerce. There has been extensive neglect of infrastructure with weakened bridges, crumbling roads, closing schools, and diminished numbers of healthcare facilities as clinics close and mental health facilities are shut down. There are reports of mine shafts violating safety laws and weather-related tragedies befalling homes built on flood plains. All of this occurs while the profits of the descendants of freeholders do not suffer commensurately.

These realities illustrate a tension evident since the founding of the nation that continues to influence our national life. Because the real costs of democracy are rarely considered in the making of rules, the operational expenses of national life are underfunded. The short-sighted dogma embraced by the powerful is to reduce spending needed to maintain democracy's house. In the American South there is a phrase used to describe houses in disrepair. The owners are considered "too poor to paint and too proud to whitewash!" This is too often the story in America, where paint peels, buildings deteriorate, children are hungry, people are sick, and minds are wasted. And if there is complaint from the millions who are harmed by such conditions, those of the freeholder mindset who hold both power and influence say the cutbacks in maintaining democracy's house are necessary because the operating costs for living in this republic are too high.

America needs to use far less whitewash, and instead spend substantially on getting the house back in order. The value of unalienable rights cannot be negotiated and requires rent payments once the rental obligations are established. To make this calculation easy, Americans should accept the fact that each year the country collects more than three trillion dollars in taxes. It is perfectly reasonable that rental income should provide additional dollars annually for meeting all the lease costs of democracy.

### *Appreciating the Value of Democracy's Lease Obligations*

It can be almost guaranteed that when "tenant" obligations for democracy's leases are added to taxes, some citizens may choose to abandon their birthrights and citizenships to void their lease. And if some should choose to leave, they should be free to do so while knowing that future economic success arising from holdings in America would still be subject to government-mandated lease obligations. It is preferable to have tenants who believe in democracy, equality, and maximum educational opportunities so that all can wisely contribute to decisions in the best interests of America. Those who do not share such ideas should go elsewhere and see if they can discover comparable levels of freedom in other parts of the world.

Like all of my classmates in New Jersey, I had no understanding of what other lands might be like except by looking at pictures in the National Geographic. The world beyond America was totally unknown. Indeed, even America with its different regional cultures was unknown to me as a child. In elementary school, I could not have imagined Africa would become a central part of my life. Eventually, my academic study, research, work assignments, and teaching were bound up in the change occurring in sub-Saharan Africa as dozens of new countries tried to cope with the challenges of independence in turbulent times.

More than two dozen trips totaling almost twelve years and spread over more than five decades gave me a deeper understanding of change in places where freedom was uncertain. I was in

Kenya as it became a republic, saw first-hand the deprivation in Alexandra township in Johannesburg during apartheid, had close-up experiences of the Amin regime in Uganda, and witnessed the growth of lawlessness in more recent decades as populations exploded and politicians learned how to use corrupt practices to become wealthy. In the epicenter of HIV/AIDS in the Rift Valley of Kenya or the Buduburam refugee camp in Ghana where Liberians survived for twenty years, no "rent" was collected in such conditions as the blessings of independence were sparse. Being in such places, however, deepened my appreciation of the gifts of freedom and equality we enjoy each day as citizens of our country. When Americans return from abroad, they all should each give thanks for the conditions embedded in our form of government that makes our lives so unique.

### *The Potential Achievements from Democracy's Rent*

The fulfillment of our individual rent obligations, our stewardship payments, can contribute to the achievement of four significant conditions vital for the future of America. But it would be wise to focus on maintaining the property and end whitewashing. Democracy's house needs:

- A clean and well-protected environment dedicated to conditions that will permit the next ten generations to live full, healthy, productive lives
- A comprehensive overhaul of the national public infrastructure accomplished without further erosion of the national economy by accumulating debt
- A notable improvement in educational standards at all

levels to permit America to rise in the rankings of academic performance when compared internationally, producing educated citizens who are second to none in the capacity to innovate and ensuring the American position in global economic affairs is without peer

- Provision of comprehensive healthcare for every American, of any age and income, that achieves the lowest possible costs in pharmaceuticals, medicines, medical treatment, and long-term care.

## *Rent and the Eye of Democracy's Needle*

Long ago when a weary traveler approached an ancient city in the dark of night he had to leave his camel or horse behind as he squeezed through the "needle's eye" in the city gates. Now our goal should be for all citizens of both great wealth and modest means to voluntarily pay their full rent and, if necessary, voluntarily give of their assets so all can squeeze through the "eye of equality" in democracy's needle and find safety and security. Those who possess great wealth need to set an example by willingly contributing their rent to ensure freedom and equality are preserved for all who reside here as citizens, legal residents and new arrivals from foreign shores for whom the lady with the lamp holds up her beacon. As good stewards of democracy's house, they will ensure the strength of this land and they will enjoy the respect and rectitude which we all seek as we walk among fellow citizens who must be equal in their commitments to the ideals to be practiced here.

# Part Six:

# Political Prescriptions

# *'Tis the Season'*
## Warnings We All Must Hear!

The television show *Million Dollar Movie* on WOR-TV in New York became popular in the 1950's by replaying a film every night for a week so a wide audience could see it in the age before VCRs, DVDs, and digital media. At Christmas time, the movie was always *Scrooge*, the 1951 version of Charles Dickens's *A Christmas Carol*, with Alistair Sim as Ebenezer Scrooge. Today, I believe the film remains the best portrayal of a tale of spiritual redemption in which the spirit of Christmas invests in the affairs of humankind. After six decades, I still watch a DVD of the film on Christmas Eve after returning from candlelight services. I find it is best viewed when fortified with brandied eggnog and a plate of sugar cookies.

As the story draws to a conclusion, Scrooge confronts the Ghost of Christmas Present, and pleads he is too old to change his behavior even if he could. The Spirit beckons to Scrooge to come closer. Quoting from Dickens's text, the confrontation between Scrooge and Spirit unfolds as follows:

> "From the foldings of its robe, it brought two children; wretched, abject, frightful, hideous, miserable. They knelt down at its feet, and clung upon the outside of its garment.

`Oh, Man. look here. Look, look, down here.'
exclaimed the Ghost.

They were a boy and a girl. Yellow, meagre,
ragged, scowling, wolfish; but prostrate, too, in
their humility. Where graceful youth should have
filled their features out, and touched them with
its freshest tints, a stale and shriveled hand, like
that of age, had pinched, and twisted them, and
pulled them into shreds. Where angels might
have sat enthroned, devils lurked, and glared
out menacing. No change, no degradation, no
perversion of humanity, in any grade, through all
the mysteries of wonderful creation, has monsters
half so horrible and dread.

Scrooge started back, appalled. Having them
shown to him in this way, he tried to say they
were fine children, but the words choked
themselves, rather than be parties to a lie of such
enormous magnitude.

`Spirit, are they yours?' Scrooge could say no
more.

`They are Man's,' said the Spirit, looking down
upon them. `And they cling to me, appealing from
their fathers. *This boy is Ignorance. This girl is
Want. Beware them both, and all of their degree,
but most of all beware this boy, for on his brow I*

> *see that written which is Doom, unless the writing*
> *be erased. Deny it.'* cried the Spirit, stretching out
> it hand toward the city. 'Slander those who tell it
> ye. Admit it for your factious purposes, and make
> it worse. And abide the end."

With those words, Dickens's story speaks to us across nearly two centuries, bringing undeniable focus to the reality of our times. Even more than the intellectual poverty too often found in our nation's schools, we must fear ignorance in all of American society. Dickens saw the poverty of the spirit in those who control society and remain profoundly uncaring of the conditions of the least of those among us. Dickens drew attention to the desperate need for dissipating the uncaring ignorance embedded in the hearts and minds of the freeholder class.

The image of impoverished ignorance among the wealthy is revealed by the wretched girl at the spirit's feet, symbolizing the want shared by millions of children who go to sleep hungry each night. Their "stale, pinched and shriveled condition" remains unrelieved as a "perversion of humanity" in our land, a land that has promised equality to all who have gathered in democracy's house. We know full well that such degradation will not be eradicated without the removal of the ignorance that compounds the tragedy.

The impact of the three spirits of Christmas on Scrooge brings about the ultimate redemption of an aging miser's metaphorical passage through the "eye of equality" in "democracy's needle" and transformation to being a good steward of equality in an era when constitutional guarantees were yet to be embraced in Victorian England or ante-bellum America. In my youth and across all the years since, *A Christmas Carol* remains a warning from the mid-nineteenth century that the basic values of life, liberty and the pursuit of happiness for all are still not fully realized. Each December 24th, the black and white images of an old film reaffirm to me the fragile condition of our democratic experiment in governing that still needs improvement but remains a light for the rest of the world, which must not be extinguished.

# *Lessons to Keep*
## Considering the Possible

The essays shared here are an introduction to the complexities of political behavior and political practice. They combine observations on how America might be redeemed with the realization of how difficult it would be to shift the narrative toward productive change and the conflict resolution that has persisted since the founding of the nation. Today, our lives are lived in conditions of serious imbalance in favor of the wealthy at the expense of the rest. Reform is clearly needed. We also know how our politics are controlled by politicians driven to pursue power and shape outcomes to realize personal goals. This is our reality.

If America is to change, it needs to focus on a very short agenda. That agenda requires fulfillment of just two fundamental initiatives to produce a meaningful impact on the lives of all Americans. If those two initiatives were to dominate the political discourse, a host of other issues would either be solved or diminished in importance. These are: (1) paying rent, and (2) winning the education war.

### *Collect All the Rent*

America cannot flourish in an environment where debate centers on ways to reduce the obligations of stewardship for those who have been enriched so exceptionally by the blessings of liberty in this country. The gap between the rich and those in the middle class cannot continue to widen. This economic chasm contradicts the well-founded principle that strong nations must have a strong middle class. The concentration of wealth among such a small percentage of the population weakens the whole country.

Americans who have prospered in this land must be willing to accept larger obligations of stewardship on behalf of the country. People are entitled to acquire as much wealth as they can within the constraints of the law. That is a freedom that should not be compromised. However, I would argue that great wealth is in part a result of the conditions from leasing a permanent residence in our democracy. The costs of this lifetime lease should be indexed by the degree a person's residence in America has conferred success on each man or women. Financial success demands the individual citizen to provide greater measures of financial stewardship by paying a higher rent.

The total annual rent payments should be of such magnitude as to ensure balanced budgets, robust surpluses for emergencies like natural disasters or threats to the national well-being, and release of the rule-makers from the pressures imposed by the "money-changers" in the temples of democracy.

### *Win the Education Wars*

America is engaged in a global war touching every branch of knowledge, including national security, economic success, technological superiority, and the biological imperative to preserve environmental viability in our land where changing conditions now make 500-year rains annual events. Winning the war requires expenditures that exceed the annual defense budgets. This is a war to be fought on many fronts, both domestic and foreign. The war must support each teacher in each classroom as they equip all children with the knowledge, insight, skills, and awareness to prevail against all forces both internal and external that can threaten the nation. In combination, fighting this war at home and abroad must be the sure defense to maintain democracy, our American way of life, and the liberties and freedoms we cherish.

This reference to liberties and preservation of freedom defines the second front in our education war if the doom Dickens's spirit character foretold is to be avoided. Our educational system can no longer neglect the importance of civic awareness and understanding. The American people must know why the rent is due and why the education war must be fought. They must know how political life functions and how governing requires constant attentiveness to national strength. That attentiveness is achieved in part by the superiority of intellectual vigor applied in the national interest. Ignorance is not bliss. Lack of awareness of how society operates is a terrible burden. Therefore, the second front in our great war must be focused awareness on to how citizenship education leads to the creation of a more perfect union for sustaining our republic far into our future.

### *Outcomes of Rent Collection and Educational Victories*

Collecting all rental payments before annual tax obligations are paid to fund the routine services that government provides will produce many positive outcomes. Our fiscal obligations will be in balance. Surpluses will routinely provide for responding to crises. The entire population will know that all Americans are paying rental costs appropriate to the degree to which they each have prospered in our democracy. The business sector will flourish, as public needs for infrastructure repair and replacement are met. Job opportunities will create more employment at home. Debt owed to foreign lands will diminish. Trade deficits may routinely become more balanced. America will finally be paying the real costs of its democratic enterprise. From such a position of fiscal strength, the nation will command greater respect in the councils of nations and in diplomatic conduct.

What the mind can conceive for this nation can be made possible. And all that is required is to accept the fact that living in our democracy incurs costs our Founding Fathers could never have imagined. However, they did provide a solution to our current needs by making wealth the standard measure for determining who might hold governing roles, and the logic for changing that condition over time as progressive philosophical beliefs encourage a governing system that is obligated to fulfill many positive responsibilities and to govern more and not less.

The evidence of educational victories will be measured by the improvement of performance in our schools, recognition of teaching as an honored and well-compensated profession, positive participation of parents in schools, rising educational standards in all states, and improved international rankings of student performance in mathematics, science, engineering, and the arts. All this will occur as a "dusted-off" version of the National Defense Education Act becomes a centerpiece of government policy to assist each state in providing resources commensurate to needs.

What else will such educational victories do for America? We will have younger generations who know their country in all of its multicultural strengths and are prepared to openly and willingly participate in a society that celebrates diversity, honors each person's right to worship as he or she chooses, respects others, and works diligently to promote the levels of cooperation among all citizens. We will also have younger generations that can take that spirit of collaboration and common purpose to engage in productive professions and pursuits that further build the strength of the country, lessening the gap that separates the wealthy from those who have so much less.

### The Narrative Must Change

Individuals who oppose paying democracy's rent and the responsibility to join the battle in America's education war will earn a title of "failed citizen patriot" for opposition undermining the future of our country. Opposition to equal opportunities for all young people is unpatriotic. The provision of educational resources, good teachers, and effective support systems must be a hallmark of every state and community. It will redeem the belief that all men and women can acquire the knowledge and insight to participate wisely in the tasks of governing and prosper according to their talents and character.

Our Founding Fathers were wise in fashioning the documents that have guided us for over two centuries. The essence of their foresight was considering that humanity could benefit from their efforts. They did not accept a notion that people were innately virtuous and good. Rather, they looked at themselves and their own foibles and shortcomings. They knew men must be constrained in their actions if the country as a whole was to flourish. They knew of the corrupting influence of power and sought to restrict the power of any one office or group. They wanted a president with limited terms, powers, and obligations to fulfill the duties of office. They wanted a body of rule-makers that represented all citizens within the constraints of a bi-cameral structure. And they wanted an independent judiciary that could intervene when rulemaking or administration of the rules seemed to breach the guarantees of the Constitution.

Changes of heart and mind will not occur if the narrative of politics and government remains unchanged. If the residual legacies of the old freeholder class are preserved despite the best efforts by the majority of Americans, then more formal legal action must require that "The rent for each man's lease on the privilege of living in our democracy is due!"

### *Keeping in Mind the Lessons Shared*

Briefly, consider the major lessons presented on these pages. The essays tell only a partial story of politics in America but have sufficient breadth to offer guidance for being a more informed citizen. The key lessons include:

## Political Basics

- Always seek to find the balance of freedom and order and whom it serves.
- Our system of governing from its founding was designed to serve the interests of the wealthy.
- Citizenship education is the key to securing fair treatment.

## Political Virtues

- Everyone is obligated to practice patriotism in every act of civic life.

- The wealthy must be challenged to become good stewards of equality.
- Voting is the baseline of citizenship.
- Denying the opportunity to vote to any qualified citizen is unpatriotic cowardice.
- Education is our greatest resource for maintaining the strength of our nation.

**Political People**

- Politicians do not accidentally appear in public life. They choose it.
- Our rural heritage significantly influenced our political traditions.
- Rural America and the values of smaller communities are still persuasive in political life.
- The family background of political people must be carefully examined.
- The values individuals pursue reveal their desire to seek power and influence.

**Political Practices**

- Our system of caucus party politics encourages stability and stifles minority views.
- Our system of voting virtually dooms effective national third-party movements.
- Politics is the process of changing or maintaining conditions through public action.
- Political victories are carried out in conflict with and at

the expense of others.
- Politicians are not reluctant to use a full arsenal of tools to achieve victories.
- Politics can be analyzed by using a handful of identifiable input and output activities, which will help produce sound judgments.

## Political Prescriptions

- Hold the warnings of the Dickensian spirit close!
- The condition of the national soul and the state of the nation must be congruent for the nation to fulfill the promises of democracy.
- Our secular faith in democracy requires willing financial support to realize ideals.
- The real costs of maintaining Democracy's House require rent for the privilege of residence throughout our lives.
- Taxes pay for the routine operating costs of our nation.

# *Acknowledgments*

The thoughts gathered here are drawn from a long career of teaching and memories of growing up in the middle of the twentieth century. Stories of my youth are woven into lessons about politics and political behavior, which are drawn from some of the best social science scholarship between the 1930's and the early 1970's. The 1950's and 1960's in particular were a rare period of change and creativity in examining political behavior as the study of politics shifted from focusing on institutions to a broader perspective of examining how people act in political situations. The ideas that have found a place in these essays owe a debt to some of the leading scholars of that era.

The most important scholar influencing my thinking was the eminent Karl Deutsch, certainly one of the leading political scientists of the twentieth century. As his student and graduate assistant, I witnessed the development of his groundbreaking work on nationalism and linking social science with cybernetics theory, as presented in his seminal work, *The Nerves of Government.* Definitions of politics, political power, and the analysis of political performance derive from his lectures and writings.

The second scholar who has had an impact on my essays is Harold D. Lasswell, whose scholarly career spanned nearly fifty years. Professor Lasswell's credentials as a medical doctor, certified psychiatrist, professor of political science, and Doctor of Law combined to make his observations on political behavior a rich landscape for examining how people decide to pursue political careers and what drives them to seek power in the public arena. Central to those ideas in this book are insights derived from Lasswell's *Politics: Who Gets What, When and How* and *Power and Society* (the latter volume written with Abraham Kaplan). Lasswell's *Psychopathology and Politics* and *Power and Personality* provide further insight into how political people act and perform.

Several other scholars influenced specific parts of this essay collection. The discussion of political parties and the limitations on creating successful third-party systems in America utilizes the ideas and observations of Maurice Duverger in his book, *Political Parties*. To develop my ideas on political religion, I relied on some of the insights of David Apter in his work, *The Politics of Modernization*. The framework for examining the various stages in assessing political issues is derived from David Easton's *The Political System*. Finally, the analysis of the choices to be made in formulating and implementing strategic campaigns to win political goals is derived from the writings of Gabriel Almond and Sydney Verba in their book, *The Civic Culture*.

Distortion or misinterpretation of the ideas and observations contained in those studies are mine alone. The more general material on the culture of the United States and the early history of the republic comes from more generalized sources on American government. Without the training in intellectual inquiry encouraged by Professor Deutsch and the writings of the aforementioned scholars, the thoughts that found their way into the lectures I delivered in the 1970's to several generations of students at St. Lawrence University would not have had the impact they had in introducing those students to the complexities of studying

American politics. The personal stories of my childhood have hopefully provided a context that calls forth memories of everyone who makes their way through these lessons about politics that I believe all Americans ought to know.

www.ingramcontent.com/pod-product-compliance
Lightning Source LLC
Chambersburg PA
CBHW032351280326
41935CB00008B/531